NORTHUMBERLAND'S
HIDDEN HISTORY

Northumberland's Hidden History

STAN BECKENSALL

AMBERLEY

First published 2009

Amberley Publishing Plc
Cirencester Road, Chalford,
Stroud, Gloucestershire, GL6 8PE

www.amberley-books.com

British Library Cataloguing in Publication Data.
A catalogue record for this book is available from the British Library.

ISBN 978 1 84868 368 6

Typesetting and Origination by Thomas Vivian
Printed in Great Britain

CONTENTS

Acknowledgements   6

Preface   7

1   Off the Alemouth Road   10

2   Ways to Waterfalls   33

3   To be a pilgrim   50

4   Seascapes   75

5   The beauty and sadness of desertion   90

6   Stone and landscapes   111

7   'The paths of glory lead but to the grave' 138

8   What's in a name?   145

9   The track now taken   155

     Bibliography   158

     Index   159

ACKNOWLEDGEMENTS

I am grateful to Marc Johnstone for his general map of the county, to Maureen Lazzari for inset maps and for the drawing of the Holy Island grave-slab, and to Greg Finch for his personal contribution on Dotland.

I thank Julia Grint for her perceptive comments on an earlier version of this book.

The photographs are my own, apart from those lent by Newcastle University, and the Blawearie family photographs provided by Mrs Joanne Gregor, who is a descendant of the Rogerson family who lived there and who is researching her family history.

The cover image is by Brian Kerr, a skilled independent researcher whose photographic record of prehistoric rock art is among images contributed by many like-minded people

I am indebted to Thomas Vivian for the speed and accuracy with which he prepared this book for publication.

PREFACE

The idea at the heart of this book came with an exploration of trackways that led to little-known places. This expanded to encompass buried places revealed in documents, excavations and from the air, parts of which might be seen above the ground, which acted as clues to much larger sites. Even highly visible features carry a hidden history, sometimes in a change of function. The fossil record of rocks pushes the exploration even further back, bringing us face to face with life lived millions of years ago.

Before our almost total reliance on motorised vehicles, the landscape would have been threaded with minor paths for people, and drove-roads for animal movement. Paths would have been shortcuts to home and places of work, and there is abundant evidence on the ground and in documents of how many there were. Many became redundant when conditions of life changed, especially when the land no longer required such intensive labour, and some of the survivors are deliberately kept in use, however spasmodically, by people who choose to walk as a leisure activity.

Railways, their tracks and attendant buildings, have suffered the same fate, and the ghosts of their presence remain long after the tracks have been scrapped.

My interest in following some of these paths has led me to places not easily accessible, not only places of great beauty, some remote and unvisited, but also to those which tell us much about our history both from signs on the ground and through documents of many kinds. The beginning of understanding our local history is to experience its places first-hand, places which acquire a stillness, a mystery, often becoming legendary. They speak of lives lived close to the soil, dependent on whatever was around them, an intimacy of people and place. They speak of work on and below the ground. Some lead to village sites now deserted.

Some paths are preserved, and new ones are created to give us access to our past and to places which have, as a result, increased leisure and money, for some have answered a demand for new exploration.

Every part of this landscape has been affected by people, whether it was to grow food or to exploit it industrially. Some parts of the county have left us a 'fossilized' record of how life might have been lived, as no one has wished to live there since these places were abandoned. This book explores a few of these places, and the significance of what remains not only to our understanding the past but also to our enjoyment of such sites physically. Into this will come some areas that I have explored already, but now some other aspect catches my eye. Some places have an inexhaustible interest.

I do not aim at being coldly rational; the forces and emotional experiences that have created me are the same as those affecting everyone. Times are different, opportunities different, but we all develop some conclusions about life and principles that must be shared; it does not matter that someone is not going to see things in the same way.

In writing this I am aware of all those who have gone before me in a similar exploration of time and place, but I hope that I have added something of myself.

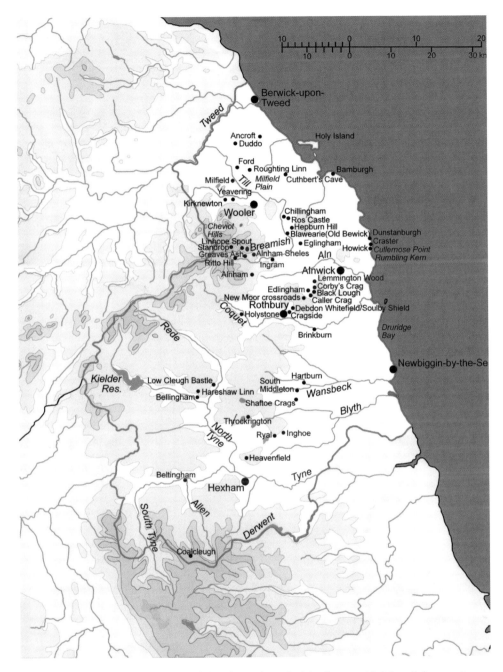

Northumberland, showing many of the places described in the text (© Marc Johnstone)

1

OFF THE ALEMOUTH ROAD

Two roads diverged in a wood, and I –
I took the one less travelled by,
And that has made all the difference.
(Robert Frost, *The Road Not Taken*, 1916)

Many of us feel at home with the familiar and do not like to venture far from the most accessible places. Others may find 'pleasure in the pathless woods … society where none intrudes'. We may come to know every bend in a well-travelled road, but there is the temptation to follow an intriguing side-road; one such is off the 'Alemouth Road' from Hexham to Alnmouth (the difference in spelling reflecting diversity of pronunciation) which takes us to a place called Thockrington. Here we will discover a church perched high on a crag of whinstone: dominant, a silent sentinel over a deserted village. Originally Norman and dedicated to St Aidan, it was probably built by the Umfraville family who were descended from those who came over with the Conqueror. It was confiscated from them early in the thirteenth century by the Archbishop of York, for violating the liberty and peace of Hexham Priory and damaging the Archbishop's land. In that century it had 18 taxpayers.

Like so many other buildings, little remains of its original structure except a tunnel-vaulted chancel, its east end now supported by massive diagonal external buttresses. But what meets the eye immediately is its double bell-cote and stone roof, seemingly built from older, reused stone. The building was constructed so that it dominates grassland that spreads for miles around, now used as grazing for animals, but once used to grow grain, as shown by the rigs and furrows picked up by oblique sunlight. To the east the land drops sharply away – hence the massive buttresses needed to support the wall – and we are overlooking the working farm. Enclosed by a wall, the church yard has graves in their original positions. These include that of Lord Beveridge who contributed so much politically to our Welfare State and who died in 1963. There is a socketed limestone base of a cross, and another stone with a carved leg of a monster on either side. Early memorials to the dead include a slab

1 St Aidan's church, Thockrington

with an incised bugle (symbol of a forester – the bugle represents a hunting horn) and a broken limestone slab, erected in the thirteenth century, that once bore a brass plate with an inscription to William and Margaret Fossour (or Fosseur), a family that settled in Thockrington at an early date, the first appearance of their name being at Swinburn in the early thirteenth century. Inside the church is a mutilated effigy of a fourteenth-century lady, wearing a wimple and curious headdress, and with a long mantle fastened across her neck with a cord.

Immediately we see that the place was not always the backwater that it appears to be today. Some lands in the area were held by the Knights Hospitallers, as we know from a survey made after the Dissolution of the Monasteries.

The parish, four miles long from north to south and two and a half from west to east, was divided into four 'townships': Thockrington, Carrycoats, Sweethope and Little Bavington, almost all of it pasture land. Centred on the church, the fields to the north have engaging names recorded in 1716, including: Park, Mead Bog, Night Fold Meadow, Mill Flat, Dodrige, Blackhill, Huckstaff, Delphs Meadow and Pool Wash. Within this area were four houses occupied by tenants, barns, stack yards, and pasture for 154 steers.

To the east there were six houses with tenants, named as George Atkinson, George Harle, Mary Buge, Jesse Steel and David and Roger Barker. The fields here included Kellhill, Whitfield, Staneford Lands and Greenwell Bogg. To the west were four houses, barns, stackyards and pasture for 60 steers, let to John Brown, William Bewick, Thomas Bird and William Maugham. There was a close called Lord's Mead.

2 Gravestones and landscape to the south

3 The abandoned settlement north of the church

Although the emphasis is entirely on pasture now, it was not always so; the extensive rig and furrow plough lines were for cultivating grain, as you can see clearly in the surrounding countryside. This was a system of ploughing with a team of oxen, making inverted S-shaped strips up and down the field, with high ridges and deep furrows that acted as drains. When the land was no longer needed to grow crops and reverted to grass, the rigs and furrows were fossilised. It looks as though the land has been ordered with a giant comb.

Unless we are prepared to look around us we may not take the track at all, but having done so it is a fine thing to know the names of the fields around us because the field names help to personalise the landscape, for the whole process of naming them reflected the intimacy between farmers and their land, sometimes incorporating their own family names, sometimes commenting on the quality and use of the soil or on the natural vegetation and wildlife. I have spent years studying these things, but the pursuit of such knowledge is never-ending. For example, there are many Night Folds throughout the county, where beasts were penned safely for the night. According to the names, there is some boggy land, meadows, a flat of land belonging to a mill, a ridge named either after Dod or meaning 'a hill'. Pool Wash may be the place where sheep were dipped, but Huckstaff doesn't give itself away. The Staneford Lands had a stone ford, the green spring had boggy ground around it. As for the people named as tenants, their familiar local names are carried on today. So how many people continued to live in the hamlet of Thockrington after 1716, when it became part of the Shaftoe estate? Records show that it had one farmhouse building and two cottages; to the north of the farm were the ruins of a bastle house (a fortified house typical of the Borders, from when self-protection was at a premium, before this turbulent area began to settle after James VI of Scotland became James I of England in 1603, thus uniting the crowns).

The village survived and in 1666 the Hearth Tax listed 11 houses. In the eighteenth century the bastle ruin had thick walls, small windows and was heavily bolted, and nearby were several grass-grown mounds forming several enclosures which acted as night folds, but as yet I have been unable to find the site of this ruin.

By 1848 there were only four farms left, and a major depopulation seems to have taken place before that. An article in the 'Proceedings of the Society of Antiquaries of Newcastle' in 1899-90 records that 'Within the living memory of the fathers now living, a village of 25-30 stood on this bleak site – around and below the church on this Whinstone crag'.

When the census became obligatory we begin to get a much more detailed picture of where people lived, where they came from and what their work was. Between 1801 and 1891 the population varied in the township, between 51 and 35 at either end. The highest number of people was 71 in 1831, the lowest was in 1891. There must be many more people buried in the graveyard who have no memorials. We always see history as fragmentary, an incomplete record, but we are given glimpses to bring us as close to it as we can get in a place like this.

What we can still see is that the church overlooks rectangular building foundations and garths (yards) of an abandoned village to the north. So the church, like others in Britain, no longer serves a clustered community, but has a shared vicar for occasional services.

4 A detail of the overgrown settlement walls

Nowadays, the road from the farm past the church to the grassland is gated and narrow, eventually reaching the old Roman road (Dere Street) now followed by the A68, to the west. It is raw, exposed country. Thus we have started a search for diversion from the main road, and have found a dominant site with a number of stories that we would otherwise have missed. We leave the place with a reflection on how Thockrington got its name: written *Thokerinton* in 1223, it was a settlement named after *Thoker*, an Anglian. As I write, it is part of another historical process, with indignation roused locally over a proposed windfarm nearby.

Onward...

The road winds along its ancient course, or sometimes runs in straight stretches where it has been enclosed by landowners and no longer has to take heed of ancient boundaries. A few milestones hide in the verges as the route runs from Hexham, a road built as a turnpike with fixed charges along the way to pay for it, linking farms with a better road heading for the port of Alnmouth, from which corn was exported: thus its title, 'The Corn Road'. There is abundant visual evidence of large fields of curving, deep rigs-and-furrows from medieval farming and of more recent, closer packed, straighter rigs – all for the growth of grain. We could pause anywhere to examine these ancient fields: at Bavington for example, but we press on past Kirkharle, birthplace of Capability Brown, past Wallington, over the beautiful but now scarred Paynes Bridge with its dramatic central arch. We continue through a landscape that includes many rocks and soils of the Carboniferous period, penetrated in parts by commercially exploited dykes of whinstone, over little hump-backed bridges that cover the remains of railway lines from Morpeth to Rothbury. Simonside begins to dominate our view on the horizon, and there are turnings to hills and sites of great scenic and historic interest such as Lordenshaw that we will bypass on this occasion. Instead we will drive through Rothbury, past Cragside, where part of the moor was completely transformed by the power of money: lakes, plantings, paths and roads centre on an extraordinary house built in a jumble of architectural styles. This is the Victorian estate of the industrial magnate Lord Armstrong, a representative of that fertile and exciting time when people of many backgrounds and disciplines shared ideas which made Britain the 'Workshop of the World'. In streams close to the ancient settlement there are little dams made from stone and wood, arranged so that water should build up to be released into Armstrong's lakes; he effectively altered the whole drainage pattern of the area to power generators so that his was the first house ever to have its own electric light. They also powered his hydraulic system used for silage production, for turning the spit in the kitchen and for running a lift to impress his guests. It is a reminder that we use what is around us to live, whether it is for subsistence or to create a surplus so that we can live in luxury.

We move on to heather-covered high moorland, leaving behind the vista of the Coquet Valley and its backing of sandstone hills. We reach Debdon Whitefield, a farm fringed by woods and straight-sided enclosures.

There are very few places to park along the Alnmouth road to give access to the next site. There is a small off-road car park at Debdon to the left, some distance away from the starting point, and there is one opposite the entrance to Debdon Pit Cottages. Access to the large grazing area that borders the road is between the Cragside estate fence that separates woodland from pasture. (The gate at the corner of the field is at NU 0715 0380).

The field is green with many mounds and slight depressions, the remains of bell pits from which coal was taken. In parts it is boggy. If there are animals in the field, keep to the fence line which leads up to the Soulby Shield small crag running roughly parallel to the road. The only tracks here are made by sheep.

The views from the crag are splendid, especially towards the Simonside hills, but it also overlooks an area of cleared land that was probably pasture in prehistoric times. Around the crag are boulders and other scree like a skirt, but towards the road are overgrown burial cairns of the Early Bronze Age, about 4000 years ago.

The ridge is covered with patches of exposed outcrop and large stones moved by ice or by people. Some have been placed upright as standing stones, chosen for their already-fluted shapes. At the south-east end of the ridge the land slopes gently to a heather-covered area with burial and clearance cairns rising obscurely from heather, and here is a small cluster of prehistoric houses. It is likely that the standing stones were erected to mark the significance of the site as a burial ground hundreds of years before the huts were built. The 'village' must represent a small stock-rearing and hunting community which may have cut grass for hay and perhaps grown tough cereals. (The settlement is at NU 080 034).

5 A 4000-year-old burial mound at Debdon Whitefield

6 A naturally eroded standing stone looking towards Simonside

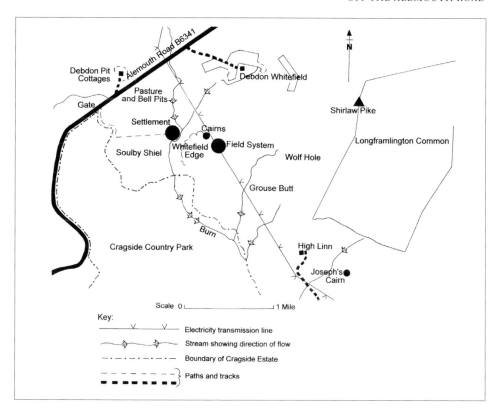

MAP I Debdon Whitefield (Maureen Lazzari)

The walk along the ridge brings you to an outstanding view of all these features, but you will need to tune in to the subtleties of the landscape to read these signs. There are two burns that meet at the far end of the heath, marked by a natural prominent knoll. The burn flowing in from the north-east defines the edge of the settlement, with the largest roundhouse slightly higher than the others, which are enfolded by a low wall in an arc that forms the back wall of the houses, with their entrances facing away from it. Everywhere you tread you will feel small and large stones under the heather with your feet, some scattered, but some following lines of walls. There are depressions made by the house bases, and changes in vegetation where the huts were 'dug' rather crudely many years ago. It looks anything but a village, but with careful attention to detail, you can work it out. It is not easy to distinguish burial cairns from field clearance heaps where they are heather-covered, but some of the larger mounds are clearly the former.

At the meeting place of the streams below the knoll there is a small dam and signs that the stream has been straightened and made to flow in a direct channel.

This is probably the work of the builders of Cragside to direct a good flow of water to artificial lakes, such as Nelly's Moss, to provide water for Lord Armstrong's hydraulic schemes at Cragside house. The knoll has been disturbed, with perhaps

7 A circular hut base, seen as a depression

some planting. The stream course is attractively self-seeding principally with silver birch trees, which thrive in acidic and damp conditions.

All in all, it is a remarkable place, hard to believe that it is so close to a main road. Across the stream lies a line of pylons above the Whitfield Edge crag to the south, and the line of their path runs over another prehistoric field system and burial cairns. South of Longframlington Common is another such settlement and village, owing its survival to the fact that the land was not attractive for arable farming and has been allowed to stay as heather moorland. The settlement that we are visiting is not alone. We will never know how many similar settlements have been destroyed by forestry, but we can at least ensure that the survivors remain as a part of our past.

To return to the ridge that gave access to this land, with minimum disturbance to grazing animals, we will again observe the heather to the south, that is relatively cleared of stone near the stream, and reflect that even a small prehistoric community living here would have had a wide range for its husbandry, coming back to its village at night.

Some hut sites of a similar age have been excavated recently, and what was found there forms the basis of reconstructions like the one below.

It is interesting to think that this is where people lived and buried their dead over 2000 years ago; a life lived on the edge, with some hunting, herding, and a little crop-growing.

Here we stand on this exposed moorland, looking at these little scraps of time, with pylons in the distance, fighter planes sometimes screaming overhead, aware that if we

8 An almost-obscured curved terrace of huts

9 A reconstructed roundhouse at Butser, southern England

10 Debdon Whitefield village from the west, lying in dark heather before the trees are reached

follow the line of pylons further south-east to another field-system and cairnfield created by other prehistoric people, we can see that this moorland would have supported few people at any time in the deep past, and today the population has shifted to industrial centres, leaving the land largely to sheep. History is about change, not progress. In Northumberland we are fortunate that this abandonment has not eliminated signs of our history, and although there is no longer any such thing as a 'natural' landscape – for all has been changed by people – there is wilderness, there is beauty, and there is history under the surface that occasionally peeps above the vegetation.

A final photograph (*20*) gives us a wide view of the site from high ground. My own perception of landscape has been considerably sharpened by viewing sites from above, either from an aircraft (particularly a microlight) or by standing on a hill or hill slope.

Onward...

From this site, with permission, we might choose to walk to our next destination, to the north-east, to meet an old road that runs from Newmoor House to Framlington Gate. We can either follow the road and park at the junction of the B6341 and the A697, or follow an uphill track (at first covered with Harbottle stone chippings) from Framlington Gate, where there is parking space. The latter is the longer route, but after the walk uphill the scene opens up at the top of the hill with an extensive view of the rest of the winding, raised road as it reaches the object of our search: an old

11 The old coach road from Newcastle to Edinburgh: Newmoor crossroads

inn, with trees around it and Thrunton Crag and the Cheviot Hills as a background to the north-west. This is a very fine landscape, full of interest, little used except for grazing cattle and sheep.

The old coaching inn is on the road that ran from Newcastle to Edinburgh. Sometimes called Rimside Moor, although this name belongs to the moor to the west, it is said to be haunted. What makes this place special is that it is in an artificially created oasis in the middle of a moor, at such a high place that coachmen thought of it as the coldest on the route north. The walk up to the site in either direction reminds us of what a haul it must have been for coach and horses. Just as Blawearie (further on in the book) is specifically designed with building, walls, garden and trees where the normal vegetation was grass and heather, at Newmoor the line of the coach road and the need for a place where passengers could be given refreshment and lodging and the horses fed and watered is shown by the rectangular fields arranged on either side of the road, and the trees planted for shelter.

To the north, the road passes over a deep culvert (reputedly haunted by a big black pig). The plantings and walls, despite the extensive views from the line of the road, have created a shut-in feeling, quiet today despite the traffic on the modern road, with the scant remains of the inn on the fringe.

The whole hilltop offers a remarkable experience. The track, once a highway, varies between a hard surface and a rutted morass; the stream cuts deeply into the grass between rows of magnificent 150-year-old beech trees and other species that

12 Beech trees on a rectangular walled enclosure

protect each other from bleak exposure. These present superbly sculpted trunks to oblique sunshine, especially in late autumn.

One can see the modern road to the south, curving above the Millstone Burn valley, the buried Roman road known as the Devil's Causeway sandwiched between it and the coach road, crossed by sandstone outcrop and boulders that have a prehistoric trail of rock art running in different directions from all three of these later routes. There is a concentration of these 5000-year-old carvings running down to the Millstone Burn and up the scarp to Snook Bank, south-west to north-east, the burn forming a funnel between high ground and the coastal plain. More space will be given to this phenomenon in other parts of the book.

Again, the view from the air gives a broad sweep of the landscape that has all these features. From here we can see our next destination across the burn valley that connects the higher ground of the north to the lower, flatter lands running towards the sea; a kind of threshold.

Back to the inn and to the walls of the enclosures, serving as a reminder that passengers needed rest and refreshment. It is also possible, I suppose, that some of the illicit whisky distilled in the hills made its way here. There is little left of the inn itself, but some of the good-quality ashlar sandstones, quarried from a gaping hole by the trackway, show what it might have been like. Now, smaller and rougher

13 The old road and inn towards Thrunton and the Cheviot Hills

14 The site from the air

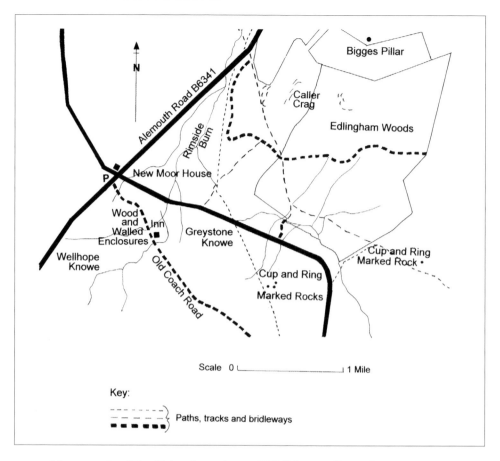

MAP 2 Newmoor Inn (Rimside) to Lemmington Hill (Maureen Lazzari)

walling stones have been added, along with some wire fencing and a rusted orange corrugated-iron roof at the gable end. Around the building, mole hills in grassland reveal many shards of white domestic pottery, of which there must be large quantities buried, but not equalling in number the thick green bottle glass fragments, especially bases, that cluster round some of the tree roots to the west.

What about the claims that the area is haunted? A fellow lecturer came to live in Northumberland after some time in Africa, bringing a dog (after a long period of quarantine) that he had rescued there. He lived in Longframlington, and used to bring his dog for a walk along this old track. The dog always refused to go into the wooded area. Another story: a sensible teacher from Alnwick who found the rock-shelter at Corby's Crag, was seated there eating sandwiches when he saw someone dressed in coachman's livery approaching. He stood up to brush off the crumbs, looked up, and the figure had vanished. I forward these experiences with no further comment.

Beekeepers bring their hives here for the bees to gather pollen from the heather, where the air is rich with the scent of heather honey. Trees now partly obscure the

15 Caller Crag from Rimside

views, but we do not have to stray far to find them. The road that we left in order to see the inn now comes in sight, to follow the scarp foot, rising steadily north-eastward on its way to Alnwick.

Onward...

To the south-east of the road the scarp rises in a series of ridges, the one for which we are aiming being Caller Crag. This could be reached from a public path that leads from Snook Bank, a farm with a name originally written as *Shakelzerdesnoke* in 1264, meaning a shackle-yard where beasts were tied on a sharp pointed ridge, through a young planted forest to Wellhope (a spring in a valley), via a track along the 'ride' in the forest which can be very boggy after heavy rain, and so to Caller Crag. Either way, you reach a place that few people are known to visit, and you are likely to be alone.

In the Wellhope wood there is an outlier of the rock carvings seen in such a concentration leading down to the Millstone Burn, a large flat rock pushing through woodland onto the grass track. Its relatively recent discovery hints that there may be others still to be found.

Sandstones have bedding planes that dictate their shapes, twisted at times, not all the layers parallel, but all created over 200 million years ago. At Caller Crag (named, as was Callaly, as a place where there were calves), wind, frost and rain have added further variety to produce remarkable shapes and textures, not only on the upstanding crags, but also on the boulders that have rolled off or been dumped there by water and the debris of retreating glaciers. Stone is a wonderful and fascinating medium, on which our imaginations can work. We can make of the shapes what we like.

16a (above), *b (below)* & *c (opposite top)* An amazing landscape of eroded sandstone at Caller Crag

Abvove 17 From Edlingham Castle and viaduct to Corby's Crag ridge

Viewed from above, the crags look across a vast landscape that encompasses valley, scarps and the Cheviot Hills on the horizon. An almost circular-fronted small cave is formed at the base of the rock where the land forms a flat shelf running in front of the crags for their whole length, providing perhaps a good place for animals to graze and be herded. On the vertical back of part of the crag is a cluster of cup marks, a signature of prehistoric people so frequently encountered in this country. There are traces of burial mounds and the ridge forms a high route along the scarp top with good visibility all round (unless there were trees to obscure the view).

The descent to the road is like a series of steps from one ridge to another, but a recently felled forest has a steeper and more jagged face. Quarrying and timber plantations occupy much of the scarp as it continues its way north-eastwards. If you wish to adventure further in that general direction, you will encounter the Black Lough at the point of Wide Hope wood, a rare small inland lake probably formed by ice sheets, and whose name means 'bleak'. For this walk you will need good strong footwear after the rather easier access to Caller Crags. We rejoin the road, which is one of the most beautifully sited in Britain. Turning again towards Alnwick we now pass Edlingham village, church, castle and railway viaduct on the west, a lovely group of monuments that are well known and visited. The church has a tower so thick that it must have been built with defence in mind, and the castle, oddly placed in a valley, is a reminder that this peaceful landscape is part of what used to be an unruly Border area.

Some of the stones of the castle may now be incorporated in the Victorian viaduct which carried the Alnwick-Cornhill railway across the valley. The rails have been dismantled, but the skilled engineering is obvious, as is the quality of its stone-built stations, many now adapted to other uses. A notable monument in Alnwick of this great enterprise is the station, long converted to use as the famous Barter Books. However, we travel the road which the railway largely superseded; the railway had its day but the road is sovereign again.

Onward…

Onwards then to Lemmington Wood, in which there is a unique survival of the past. At the top of a rise, a small minor road branches towards Lemmington Hall across the old railway track, the intersection marked by a large grassy area with a wooden seat. The wood is enclosed by a wall, and the gate leads along a public path through untidy woodland downhill to the north, once a track to the railway. To the right of this, not easy to find in tangle of rhododendron and other growth, is a rock outcrop on which 'cup and ring' marks made over 4000 years ago were hammered onto the upper surface. These were known of many years ago, but more recently researchers Irene and Ian Hewitt from Poole re-located them and found something completely unexpected on the same surface: three runes. Both sets of motifs are illustrated here.

I sent drawings and pictures of these runes to experts. They responded by explaining that runes are an alphabet, normally found on detached slabs of stone, for example on burial stones, so the occurrence of these on an outcrop is either rare or unique. They may have been part of a sacred text, and may mean either 'to

18 Runes on outcrop at Lemmington Hill

leave behind' from the Old English verb *laefen*, or 'a remnant or relic', from *laf*. An alternative is that they are Old Norse, from the noun *lof*, meaning 'praise or permission' or *laf*, meaning 'bread or sustenance'. The runes were inscribed at least 2000 years later than the prehistoric motifs, and it is possible that they were put on the same rock deliberately, even if the precise meaning of the earlier symbols was as obscure to them as it is to us, which is quite possible. The significant detail is their position, here on what may have been an ancient trackway leading from the valley up the scarp, where there are notable prehistoric monuments and structures.

If you are interested in old railways, you have a good section to explore below the wood. The name Lemmington, *Lemetun* in 1157, signifies that the farm there was named after brook-lime, or Speedwell (*hleomoc-tun* in Old English).

We can now take an unmarked route to the top of the ridge, where the Crags include a flat top where my children and I used to picnic; they called it 'Table Rock'. Little did I know that years later I would excavate an important cremation burial on the floor of a rock-shelter near there, at a place called Corby's Crag (named after a crow). To reach this site you follow a track from the road that leads through land punctuated by derelict bell pits.

From medieval times onwards, these circular collared shafts were a common way of extracting coal to a safe depth; another shaft was then dug along the seam, when it became too dangerous to exploit further downwards. There were many bell pits all over Northumberland, and they are marked on OS maps, although most of the high-grade coal for mines came from shafts along the coast. There is a fence from here marked on the map, and it is this boundary at which you aim, with a gate through the fence bringing you to the rock-shelter. It is a powerful and intriguing site – a natural dome of overhanging rock

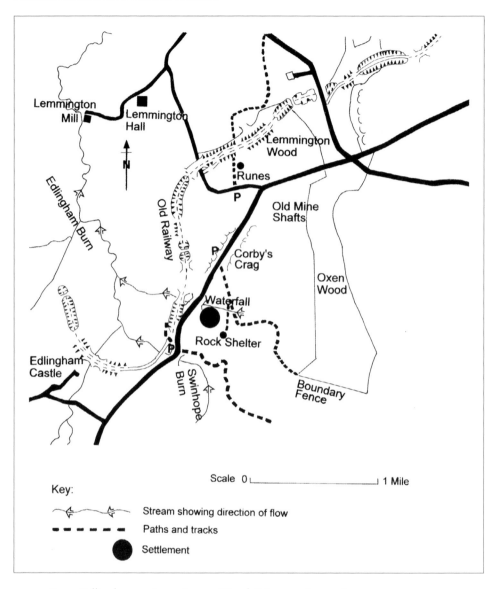

MAP 3 From Edlingham to Lemmington Wood (Maureen Lazzari)

in which the layers of sandstone are multi-coloured with iron staining. The site commands extensive views and can be seen from a considerable distance away (from the road, for example, like a large slit in the rock). It is a shelter that was used by people whose lives were mobile: by the earliest hunter-gatherers of Mesolithic (Middle Stone Age) times; by Early Bronze Age people who used the floor of the overhang to bury an upright pot full of cremated human bone, covered with a triangular flat sandstone slab; by bell pit workers or shepherds who carved a seat and little ledges and who left behind their litter – part of a penknife, teacup, clay pipe, broken glass. These last sojourners built a small wall and screen as a shelter from the wind, unaware of the dead man at their feet.

19 An abandoned bell pit

20 Corby's Crag rock shelter from the east

All of this has been thoroughly recorded (see the Bibliography) should you wish to know more, but meanwhile you will see that there are steps cut from the top of the rock to the overhang below, a swathe of stone taken out, and the initials 'S' and 'P' carved into the rock. This and the fence that continues up the hill to some very oddly placed boulders that may have acted as standing stones, marks the erstwhile boundary of Percy and Swinburn lands. Below the shelter towards the road is a concealed prehistoric settlement, largely unexplored, but probably Iron Age or Romano-British, that has a double wall enclosing it, ending at the steep scarp edge.

At the foot of this scarp where the road runs is a small waterfall, accessible from a little lay-by, where the purpose-built structure of an original tollroad bridge still bears the road. All of this is inaccessible except on foot, and it would be courteous to seek permission from the farmer to depart from paths, even with open access.

The valley which this site overlooks inspired a poem that I now offer to you. It needs no further comment:

AUTUMN GOLD

This valley holds the melting point of
gold.
Here, at the year's end, poised,
Like this scarp of grey sandstone,
Fretted with cold water running down
its cheeks,
We tremble at the edge of silence
And the hovering kestrel's path of time.
Below, a shattered castle keep
Blends with deep shadows of rich earth
As sunlight slowly strokes each tree
and field.
A subtle shift of texture threads the
cooling air
Among the gentle falling of the leaves,
The spinning of winged seeds or sigh of
brittle pine.
But far beyond the urgent change
That dying bracken at our feet foretells,
Grey rounded Cheviots snuggle closer
to warm clouds,
While all the space between is
indistinct,
Simmering in a crucible of westering sun,

Still glowing gold, dark green and
brown,
With flames of scarlet licking round.
The store of summer drains away
To leave an aching sadness for the
richness that was there.
Cold realisation of our loss
Throbs slowly through the current of
our blood;
We touch the solid rock for reassurance
That next year will be the same,
And after that … and after that …
Who knows what follows?
Our bodies cry inside, 'Stay, stay. Come
back. Come back'.
Yet even as we watch,
The sun-shift and the lengthened
shadows
Drag away the hope
That we can catch and keep the beauty
of this place for ever.
Soon, all this valley will be drained of
life.

So we leave the course of this fascinating road at a place where the landscape slowly begins to change in character as it approaches Alnwick and the coast.

2

WAYS TO WATERFALLS

Northumberland is not a landscape of dramatic waterfalls, but it has three modest falls in secluded places that have considerable charm and magic; although the falls themselves are fairly well-known, their wider landscape and historical settings may not be. Coincidentally, the name of each one incorporates the word 'Linn', a dialect word for pool. The Welsh *llyn* means water, although in some names it comes from Old Scandinavian *lin*, meaning flax. Hareshaw Linn has a waterfall that empties into a pool from the Hare ridge; Roughting Linn bellows like a bull, and Linhope Spout is a spout of water falling into a pool in a blind valley. They are in different parts of the county: the central sandstone region, the northern scarpland and the volcanic Cheviot Hills. Although the falls themselves are well-known, their wider landscape and historical settings may not be.

HARESHAW LINN

Hareshaw Linn lies in the upper reaches of a stream with the same name. The water pours over an overhanging cliff into a steep-sided valley that in section reveals hard sandstone overlying weaker shales. The moving water is wearing these away at different rates; the bed of the stream has great blocks of broken-off sandstone, but the shale turns to silt and is more easily swept along. It is a continuous process, so that in time more blocks will fall off and the waterfall will move further upstream, lengthening the gorge in the process.

The swift flow of water cuts down into the bed of the stream, working it away, falling over rocks that have the greatest resistance as mini waterfalls, so that little rushes of sound meet us as we move along the banks. The force of the water has created a steep-sided valley that is visually and aurally concentrated, different from the world outside it. This makes it special, for it has given birth to its own ecosystem of plant and animal life, making a walk along the burn exciting and interesting.

Today the valley is looked after by the Northumberland National Park, making it more easily accessible and safer than it used to be. Although its length is still a long ramble and

21 Hareshaw Linn waterfall, Bellingham

occasionally a slippery one, it has some cobbled sections of path and several small bridges that take us in a zigzag course from bank to bank towards the object of our journey, the main waterfall. We will need to return the way we came, the same way that the people took in the 1890s, though now with more cobbles and more bridges.

It is easy to see why this is a place of Special Scientific Interest; packed into the gorge is a diversity of trees that includes oak, ash, birch, hazel, willow, cherry, douglas fir and rhododendron, all home to many birds and to red squirrels. There are ferns, mosses and flowers in abundance and a wide range of fungi thrive upon fallen trees and rich decayed leaves. Autumn in particular is an active season; although everything appears to be dying there is considerable life flourishing among plants and creatures that benefit from the death of others. The unpleasant smell of the stinkhorn intrudes into the more pleasant dead-leaf, chestnut smell of the valley floor; it too must live and propagate – by having a vile odour to attract the flies that will carry its spores.

Not for the first time I am faced by the conundrum of Creation by an all-loving Deity, for what is superficially so beautiful hides a cycle of destruction and horror. The lovely blackbirds and thrushes devour caterpillars, worms and snails. The tawny owl sweeps around for its innocent prey. The wood mouse and vole, both vegetarian, are hunted by predators. Beetles, spiders and ants feed on a variety of smaller insects. The balance of Nature, as decreed by its laws, ensures that death and decomposition work in its favour. One is seldom aware of this during a walk in such a beautiful

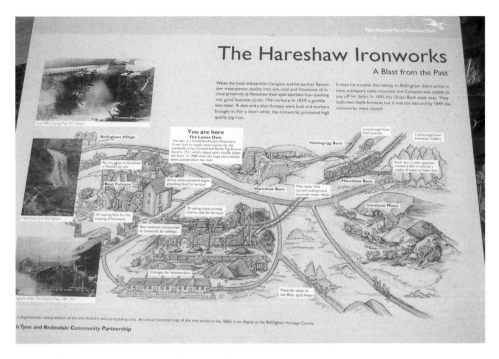

22 Display board at the car park

valley, as the struggle is mostly invisible except to those who look specifically for it under decayed trees or in the undergrowth. I remember when a boatman on the Moray Firth who was showing us the delightful antics of dolphins suddenly commented on the 'hell' that existed under the surface of the water – something which a whole series of televised programmes has since brought so vividly to our notice. Do we accept that 'whatever *is* is *right*', as Alexander Pope put it? Perhaps we should put such considerations behind us when we enter the magical valley.

The starting point for the walk is not particularly easy to find: it branches from a road in Bellingham village, where there is a car park alongside the ambulance station. Turn off the main road opposite the Police Station (following the sign to the Heritage Centre), then take the first left alongside the stream.

Not just any old car park, though, for here there used to be a large iron-works that employed 500 people, including those who brought in the coal and iron ore to the industrial complex. The works included a water wheel, fed by leading water underground from the burn by use of a specially constructed dam (the impressive remains of which will be seen upstream), which powered the bellows of a blast furnace. In a short-lived operation of only ten years, raw nodules of iron were dug out of local clay, roasted in 24 kilns by coke produced from 70 coking ovens from coal mined locally, some of which was brought to the site by a little steam engine; some of the rails from this line still languish in the valley. The pig iron produced here went to Hexham to be processed. The big problem of the enterprise, which housed its

23 The latest bridge to be built at Hareshaw

workers in homes built of local stone, was transport; the construction of the railway and the station, now occupied by the Bellingham Heritage Centre, was too late to save it and it finally closed in 1849.

Most of the buildings have gone; as with so many old industrial buildings in Northumberland they were swept away, their materials re-cycled, leaving little trace. However, our walk along the burn side is immediately marked by subtle signs of what used to be: here coal and iron were dug out, there slag was dumped in mounds, all now blending with the landscape, reclaimed by plants and animals. Since there is also limestone in the sedimentary rocks, the disturbance of mining threw out some lime-rich soil favoured by plants that would otherwise not have thrived here. Early on in the walk along the burn there is a more defined survivor of our industrial past – a dam, marked by a display board. This dam has survived two floods, in 1911 and 1968. An additional supply of water came from the construction of an earth dam two miles further upstream, and there are plans afoot to reveal more of this industrial heritage. If only more time were given to improving our current manufacturing capacity, then we might not feel that we are increasingly living in a museum.

About five years ago the final one of the little wooden bridges over the burn, built to make it easier for us to walk the valley, was brilliantly designed and rebuilt.

Its curves and interlacings contrast with the other bridges, putting one in mind of a scene from the mind of Tolkien. Local people have recorded that at the sixth of the bridges the late Victorians used to hold parties, even constructing a special area for the events. It is recorded in Bellingham Heritage Centre that:

> In Victorian times big picnics were organised … and music played … the violin and the accordion. There was a lovely spring and they would light a fire and make tea. They cut a terrace for this out of the bankside.

My photographs were taken on one sunny day in the very late autumn of 2006, on the ninth of November. During my walk I met only three couples and three Park Wardens who were examining the condition of the trees, being particularly concerned with what to do about the dead wood. Modern forestry favours allowing fallen and dying trees to remain and to decay, as this encourages mini-beasts, so that what might seem untidy to some is 'life in all its abundance' to others. The colours were remarkable, especially those of the fallen leaves and of those remaining on the trees suspended over the water, reluctant to fall. Hawthorn berries, especially from bushes growing on the industrial mounds, were spectacularly red; nearby silver birch had a profusion of delicate leaves that shimmered in a slight breeze on higher ground. Within the gorge the fallen trees of long ago were thick with fungus, while some of the upright trees had bracket fungus in light steps up the trunk. Victorian-planted Douglas fir were a contrast, with their dark, erect trunks among the gold, red and orange of beeches, at their most beautiful at that time of year. Trees grow at all levels in the gorge, dominating the top of the sandstone outcrop, covering the slopes, clinging wherever they can, and lining the bottom. There is no uniformity; variety is what makes this valley so rich in texture and colour.

Bellingham is the centre of an area with varied scenery and many layers of evidence of times past. As you leave the village, past the Heritage Centre towards the A68, you pass conical mounds of spoil. From this road you can see more mounds, clusters of distant cones, waste material from quarries that once provided material for the furnaces of the nearby Ridsdale ironworks, which looked more like a castle than a foundry beside the main road. This works was the source of the iron used for Lord Armstrong's revolutionary breach-loading guns, tested here, and watched by arms-buyers from all over the world.

Also off this road, on either side, are two bastle houses, called Hole and Low Cleughs. There are many of these small fortified farmhouses in Northumberland, and several others in this area such as Black Middens and Greenhaugh, but Low Cleughs Bastle is particularly worth the walk along a stream from a parking place at the side of the road. You pass through a landscape that has grassed over the ancient rig and furrow system of farming, once arable but now preserved as pasture. You see many earth and stone-dump field walls that once divided the function of different fields. The light in November is obliquely strong, when every wrinkle in the ground is visible.

The bastle itself has characteristically thick walls and looks across an extensive valley from a place near the top of the hill. It is box-like, functional, with few

24 The Hareshaw Burn valley

25 Low Cleugh bastle

concessions to light, and with a doorway that has large bolt-holes clearly chipped into the rock. The base is made of massive stones and its other stones are large. It is roofless today, and inside we can see the joist holes that show where the second floor was situated. The construction speaks of defence, for this is Border country. It was built long after the Roman Road, Dere Street, which runs close by, and which, with the fort that housed the Roman border patrols, had a different strategic purpose. Now it belongs to a vast, open landscape, with few habitations and lots of sheep. Bellingham itself rests in a more sheltered place, at the centre. Industry, abandoned railways, agriculture, power struggles, life at the edge, all are here and partly visible for those who wish to search. Hareshaw Linn provides a unique place within this vast landscape, shut in, diverse, now quiet, and full of interest. Above all, it is a place to relax and to enjoy colour and sound, to connect to a life away from television, roads, business and all to which flesh is heir.

ROUGHTING LINN

Roughting Linn has become well-known recently, mainly because it is the place where the largest prehistoric decorated outcrop in England is found. It also has a 'hidden' valley with a waterfall. The exposure of sandstone in a little gorge, some of it full of holes that occurred when it was being formed millions of years ago, has been eroded by a stream that falls from an overhang. Like Hareshaw Linn, in time this will move further upstream as the rock is undermined. The sheer-sided, not very high end of the valley has a small waterfall that is something like a stage set, the best approach for which is to walk up the stream bed. We begin at a path that leads off the narrow metalled road that leads, privately, to Roughting Linn farm, signposted as such. The land is private, but I and my friends have never had difficulty in getting permission to be there; it is, however, one of those places where it always a good and courteous idea to ask permission to view.

The path follows a steep descent to the burn, and to your right on the way down there is a strange sandstone boulder or outcrop that looks, with some imagination, like a tortoise. Trees on the slope and below it help in the descent, which ends with a widening bank of the stream that is joined a few metres away by the burn that has formed the waterfall. Together these streams flow towards the Milfield Plain. As you turn towards the fall, the trees thicken and form arches, witch-like, and the bare sandstone rock-face appears with a deep hole through it, going nowhere. It is no time at all before the waterfall and its pond appear before you.

This little gem of a place has changed little in the many years that I have known it. The sound is magnified, although the name 'roaring' is hardly appropriate, even after a downpour. Rocks in the water bear different quantities of moss each year, and branches fall in the water and are sculpted by the falls. To the left is a rock overhang, now out of reach of the fall, low over the water, but with room enough to walk or crouch beneath. I have known ducks to hatch their eggs among water-soaked cobbles here without

26 Roughting Linn waterfall

human or other disturbance. This may well have been used as a temporary shelter in the past, bearing in mind that Northumberland has rock overhangs that have been used by generations of prehistoric people, sometimes as a place for the burial of the dead or as a place out of the wind where they could shape their tools out of flint or add their motifs to the rock face or floor. This overhang has not revealed any such artefacts, but it might have been used as a temporary shelter or, more likely, it had such an atmosphere that it had a more spiritual significance. Why? First of all, if we explore what is around this fall, the land has had several uses over a long period of time. The sandstone overhang over which the water falls is a continuation of a ridge that runs from an ancient burial ground in use over 4000 years ago, but destroyed by farming. This ridge has rock art motifs along its track, leading to Goatscrag Hill, where there are dramatic overhangs with excavated burials, and flints have been found there, worked by the earliest people in Northumberland, the Middle Stone Age (Mesolithic) hunter-gatherers. On the vertical wall are depictions of four animals, probably deer, one with its legs 'in motion' and the others rigid. Despite speculation, no-one knows when these were carved, but they appear to be prehistoric. Clearly everything points to an area of some importance in the deep past. At Roughting Linn we are at a kind of crossroads, with one route leading to the North Sea and the other to the Milfield Plain, with its henges and other 'ritual' monuments.

27 Young people's art work based on prehistoric rock-art motifs

I have had plenty of opportunity to observe how people react to Roughting Linn, including children and adults on courses at Ford Castle. Adults are often awed, certainly moved, and when a group with me reported their experience to members of an Art course, an octogenarian ex-miner from Ashington was so determined to see the waterfall for himself that they arranged to help him down the slope with a rope tied to a tree. He was deeply grateful for the experience. Young people are excited by it, must cross the shallow stream to the other side, must get as close to the falling water as possible. There is no danger. For many this is the land of the exotic.

The most recent group that I took there was from County Durham. In the spring of 2004 I was asked to assist with 'a journey of exploration into the past' called 'Written in Stone'. Young people from Greenfield Community School, Newton Aycliffe, were involved in a series of workshops, Lottery-funded, and initiated by Creative Partnerships. With support from their excellent young art teachers and various specialists, the young people were put into situations where they could explore their environments and respond to them in their own way in various artistic media, including glass-making. My role was to begin the exploration with them.

Imagery was the theme, but I wanted to show them the waterfall first, without comment. It was great fun for the fourteen-year-olds to make the journey on foot to reach it, but when they arrived at the site a temporary stillness settled on them. It really was quite an extraordinary reaction: it was as though they were looking at something in a dream. This was a prelude to their first encounter with rock art hammered into the higher-placed rock, which they reached by walking over the ramparts and ditches of a settlement that ends at the edge overhanging the waterfall. When they reached the rock the sun was strong, so all of the 5000 year-old markings were intensely visible. The questions began, and they responded directly to their own experiences; no one told them what they should think.

Places are not limited to one time, but are also part of a greater history spread out in the landscape around us. Sites like this attract people for all kinds of reasons, offering different messages accordingly. Sometimes the message comes from something manufactured in people's minds, subjectively inferred so that it becomes more an extension of their own preconceptions than anything to do with the intentions of people in the past that created and venerated the sites. To respect a site used in the past we should not add to it in our casual arrogance; bits of rubbish hanging from trees hardly do justice to sites like Roughting Linn. Even worse was the occasion when someone had painted in the grooves of the ancient symbols with brown paint. The gods will not forgive them for that!

There is always a problem of access, conservation and information on sites like this. Some of us have long campaigned for intelligent 'management' of Roughting Linn, but until recently nothing was done. Now a large obtrusive fence and a ghastly crumbling Ministry of Works notice board have been removed, and growth that was threatening to split this huge whaleback of rock has been cut back. Now the rock appears as it did at the time of its first recording in the nineteenth century, as a prominent dome not hemmed in by trees. More remains to be done, of course, but some people regret the removal of the vegetation that made it a more 'secret' place.

This part of the site is stone, but water too was venerated. Archaeologists continue to discover all over Britain metal tools and weapons that have been deliberately deposited in rivers, streams and lakes. At one time these objects were thought to have been 'lost' or thrown away in a panic, but no longer: the evidence for ritual deposition is too strong. The pond at Roughting Linn in its little closed-in valley lies at the foot of an outcrop that carried multiple ditches and walls that curve in an arc to reach the promontory edge. No one knows the date of this enclosure, but parallels indicate around 2000 years ago, long after the rock art and the burials that we know about. The pre-Roman people, sometimes known as Iron Age or Celts, with their Druidic religion, and the people before them, were responsible for many water-offerings; the waterfall and pond would seem just the kind of place to attract them. After all, it was on their doorstep.

Why venerate water? Probably in part for the same complex reasons that we still find it endlessly fascinating. But if we consider that bygone people and animals would quite literally die without a natural local supply, especially if the temperature were higher at the time, a key element in all religions comes into play: we acknowledge our dependence on forces outside ourselves; we ask for their help in times of need, we offer something in return for that help. We may have given back to the water something that we valued: we thus placed our precious objects out of circulation, something that also sometimes happened when the dead were accompanied by 'grave goods'. The nature of sacrifice is that it costs us.

I know that all of this, applied to a specific pool of water, is speculative, but it is based on wide reading of what others have found – one must start with a hypothesis, and then try to understand why we formulated it. I have written a book on Northumberland called *The Power of Place* because I believe that it is true that, for varied reasons, places do move us with a sense of their importance or beauty. And water is a substance of beauty: streams, cascades catching the sunlight, rainfall and rainbows, mist and dewfall. It is a source of life, a source of radiance when illuminated with moonlight and starlight. Sun and moon form beams that seem like pathways to the heavens as they rise and set above quiet lakes and seas. Floods are awesome, dangerous when the raging beast is let loose, and lethal. Thunderstorms scare some people out of their wits when the heavens are torn apart by lightning. Rivers rise and cannot be crossed, they flood and bring death, are untamable; yet with the silt they deposit they bring new life, too. They swarm with fish. They allow us to be transported from coast to hinterland. The seas open up exotic places beyond our comprehension, where whales and dolphins break the surface above whatever lurks beneath, be it real or imaginary creatures like the Leviathan or the Loch Ness monster.

Over water come explorers, settlers, Vikings to Northumberland. Water drowns and transforms. Read how Shakespeare sees this transformation in *The Tempest*:

> Full fathom five thy father lies;
> Of his bones are coral made;
> Those are pearls that were his eyes;
> Nothing of him that doth fade
> But doth suffer a sea-change
> Into something rich and strange.

Water purifies, and many religions acknowledge this in their rites.

Water became the Christian symbol of Baptism, a cleansing and a new beginning, but it hearkened back to events such as when Moses led his people to safety across the Red Sea, and how he saved them from thirst by striking the rock with his staff, releasing the spring.

A waterfall creates perpetual sound, echoed in gorges when it cascades; an eternity of sound and movement, a truly living thing. As Heraclitus said, we can never stand in the same river twice, for all is flux, all is perpetually in motion. Water creates a life special to itself in that hidden place, with plants that grow there rather than anywhere else, a kind of micro-climate, and these plants attract the fauna that also flourish there more than anywhere else. A waterfall is also a kind of signpost, a reference point in a vast landscape crossed only by trails. Our journeys, our experiences and our destinations may differ, but we may draw something from such special places to sustain us.

LINHOPE SPOUT

Linhope Spout lies deep inside the Cheviot Hills and is usually reached through the Ingram valley, in a region shaped by the action of fire. This is a landscape of extinct volcanoes, where solid 'plugs' of rock still rise above the rounded hills, further shaped by the action of ice. After the furnace, the glaciers; after the glaciers and

28 The east entrance to the Ingram valley

the change in temperature, the colonisation by plants and animals. The core of the Cheviot Hills is granite, pink in colour with gas bubble-holes filled in with minerals that have different colours. Around the granite are other volcanic rocks: andesite and porphyrite. They are not easily identified, except in gashes, scree or in boulders on the surface, as the bulk is now covered with vegetation. This vegetation does not, however, disguise the underlying profile of the rounded hills and valleys, making it different from the sandstone scarplands that we have just visited.

The River Breamish, a pre-Roman name that probably means 'to roar', flows to the North Sea as do other Northumberland rivers. But there is a difference, for at Powburn the Breamish makes a turn northwards for a few miles, changes its name to Till at Old Bewick, and then cuts through a gap at Weetwood Bridge to enter the relatively flat plain of Milfield. Joined by the River Glen, it then joins the River Tweed further north, and at last resumes an easterly course to the sea. By then it has traversed the fundamentally different underlying geological structures of Northumberland.

The name Ingram is given to a settlement covered with grass, and indeed grass covers the agricultural terraces and rig and furrow systems that are witness to hundreds of years of arable farming. This was the case until the land became exhausted, the temperature variable, and pasturing became the answer to huge

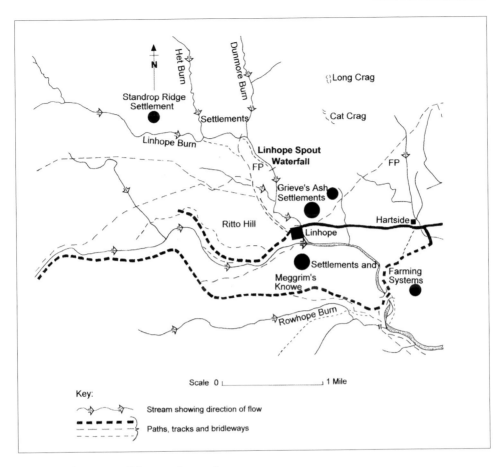

MAP 4 Linhope area (Maureen Lazzari)

stretches of land where few people wanted to live, but which would support many grazing animals. We enter this valley from the main road into Scotland, the A697, where all the signs of a fossilised prehistoric and Romano-British civilisation survive, visible to the observant, and accessible to archaeological excavators; this has long been known as one of the finest intact ancient farming and settlement areas in Britain. On the hilltops above the river there are cairns, ancient field walls and well-defined enclosures relating to people using the area for over 1000 years. From the air one can see an incredible number of settlements that have been established at different times, all clearly visible even under vegetation when the sun shines obliquely onto them, casting deep shadows. For ten years, a programme of scientific excavation has helped to separate site from site, with finds of the Middle Stone Age and later flints, Early Bronze Age burials, house sites, enclosures and long field walls of many periods that have divided up the landscape. There is evidence of defence, disposal of the dead, communication and places to live. The story of this is made easily available in the Northumberland National Park visitor centre, especially with the display of artefacts

29 Greaves Ash: remains of Iron Age and later walling, looking east

found during the excavations, so this is a good place to pause on the route further up the valley. From there you will be given guidance on what routes to follow and what to see and understand in this extensive landscape.

Part of the floor of the valley from here has deep rig and furrow systems, so much so that if you park at Boulby's Wood you may wonder why the car runs over high ridges on the grassed part of the car park. Here the valley floor is open and fairly wide, with hills on either side, and as you move further west it narrows where it is joined by a small tributary. We follow Linhope Burn further along the valley, keeping to the northern side, but before we reach our destination at the waterfall there is much to see, for we are still among prehistoric and later settlements. Perhaps the greatest of these is Greave's (or Grieve's) Ash.

For many metres before we reach it, we will be on foot walking along a road where visitors' cars are not allowed. To the right is a small wood before we reach the village of Linhope, beside which is a complex series of enclosures and roundhouse walls, with a hollow way leading into this Iron Age or Romano/British settlement. It has not been excavated in recent times, though some digging has been done there, so we don't have much reliable detail. However, with another enclosed settlement towards the east, and the two circular sites linked by linear walls and enclosures, it is in a good state of preservation, best seen when the bracken is dead. We can imagine

30 From Linhope to Brough Law and Alnhamshields

roundhouses with their tipi-like thatched roofs arranged inside a large ditched circular wall side by side with pens for their valuable animals. Comings and goings have made the road deeper each year, so that it is still clearly defined today. There is plenty of evidence around of ploughing for grain, much of the area used over and over again for centuries, with animals pastured on the less-fertile lands round about. There was plenty of water for them. Although the community is visible at ground level, it is best appreciated from the air, which is how we get the broad picture of what was happening in the past.

Further to the east on a plain was a medieval settlement called Alnhamshields, in existence in 1265, with 11 tenants remaining in 1314 but abandoned by about 1550. Its 20 rectangular buildings, contrasting with those of the prehistoric village, are still faintly visible, along with the fields that supported it. A public right of way leads to it.

All of this emphasises how people have used these upland areas to make a living for centuries, until arable agriculture gave way almost exclusively to stock rearing; this accounts for the sparsely inhabited land today, and the openness of the landscape. It is not the case that a large population must have lived there just because there are so many domestic sites visible; population density depends on how many people were living there *for a particular period*. Visible settlements may have had only a short life-span, and what we see may have been used over and over again.

31 Linhope Spout

There is an easily walked track from the village of Linhope to the waterfall, a path which continues to more of these ancient settlements and to a nature reserve which has rare plants and birds. A feature is the number of volcanic plugs and crags that protrude from the grassland. The path to the waterfall is signposted, and is quite steep in places to where the Linhope Burn cascades in a concentrated stream ('spout' being a good word to describe it) over a sudden drop in the natural rock formation.

The noise of water falling into a swirling pool is perpetual, as the burn re-forms and continues its way down the valley to the village through which we have just come. You may choose to follow the valley on a more difficult, less-defined route in the direction of the Ingram valley and the abandoned village of Alnhamshields, mentioned above.

But the waterfall is a place to stop and to consider what its impact might have been on people who lived there. It would have been an important landmark, visual and audible. It would have provided water for thirsty cattle in the summer, when at times in prehistory the temperature was higher. It may well have appeared as something miraculous, and its pool may have attracted offerings. Above all, it is another of those partly secluded places where we can enjoy feeling a difference, an experience of timelessness. We may encounter in ourselves, through all that remains, a sense of

32 The spout from the south

time and a spirit of curiosity about how other people lived their lives long before we were born. It is also a place that becomes a focal point of further exploration of this amazing landscape, depending on your fitness and sense of adventure.

In the autumn, the delicacy of massed tree branches in the valley leading to the pool is such that it looks like grey smoke amid the gold, brown, yellow and green of trees at the dying of the year. It is a reminder that places themselves change in our perception according to the time when we view them. Rain, frost, hail and snow may remind us forcibly of the bleakness there and the sheer struggle of people to survive in numerous small settlements around Linhope. It may appear beautiful to us when we don't have to make a living there. I thought this recently as I walked from the waterfall back to the modern Linhope settlement; to the right of the track on the lower slopes of Ritto's Hill, with its extraordinary all-round views of hills and valleys not completely covered by an 'Open Access' agreement, there is yet another pre-Roman village of low round stockades, walls and house sites, warmed by the sun, showing just a little of its ground plan and its extent. Shortly, winter would be on it, and people's lives would change.

3

TO BE A PILGRIM

His first avowed intent, to be a pilgrim
(John Bunyan)

Whan that Aprille with hise shoures soote
The droghte of March hath perced to the roote,
And bathed every veyne in swich licour
Of which vertu engendered is the flour ...
Thanne longen folk to goon on pilgrimages,
And palmers for to seken struange strondes,
To ferne halwes, kowthe in sundry londes.
(Geoffrey Chaucer: the Prologue to the *Canterbury Tales*)

When April with his sweet showers has pierced the drought of March to the root,
and bathed ever vein in such sap that gives life to the flower ... then folk long to
go on pilgrimages and palmers to seek strange shores in foreign lands, to shrines of
saints in distant countries. (My translation)

One of the most famous Pilgrimage routes to shrines in Britain is the Pilgrims' Way to
Canterbury, made particularly famous by Chaucer's *The Canterbury Tales*. It is one of
many in Britain, and Northumberland's own pilgrimage route is to Holy Island.

There are shrines all over Britain; some are pagan in origin, having had their
holiness established in pre-Christian times, later to be absorbed into Christianity. The
importance of water at such sites has already been mentioned in the previous chapter
in this account. Long before Celtic paganism (including the Druids), there were many
places of pilgrimage visited in prehistoric Britain, not only the great stone circles or
henges such as Avebury and Long Meg or Thornborough, but also the many circles of
timber and areas enclosed by a ditch. At Milfield, one of the excavated sites of a henge,
a ditched enclosure with a circle of posts has been reconstructed for all to see.

33 The reconstructed Milfield henge

34 The Duddo stones

There are also standing stones, single, grouped or in lines that mark important places. I offer here a poem about the importance of these stones to prehistoric people:

STANDING STONES

Rooted teeth, the hunter's hold on flesh
That once roamed free
Pursued by points of flint
Broken from the ground and shaped.

We need to rearrange the universe
To suit ourselves;
To drag stones, sometimes shape them,
Plant them in the earth
In rows, in circles, single sentinels
Enfolding, leading, isolated,
Each according to our need.
The circle pulls the sun and moon
Down from the rhythmic flow of sky,
Ensuring that their magic works for us.

Stone rows lead the rising and the setting of the sun,
An avenue of our own creation,
And when crops fail, beasts sicken,
Fever strikes and children die,
Our faith is vested in recycled rock
Born of the earth but pointing to the sky,
Invested with acknowledgement
That without god's assistance
We are but specks of dust, and powerless
Within the vastness of a universe.
Stones, planted properly will help our crops to grow.
Stones guarantee the flow
Within bow's reach or slingshot's range
Of beasts that clothe and nourish us.
When nature fails us,
Bringing death, disease, the breaking up of tribes.
We do not blame the stones,
But offer them new bribes.

There are thousands of circular burial mounds, some of which still survive, especially on poorer soils where modern farming has not destroyed them. We know a little

35 Blawearie excavated cairns

about how prehistoric sites of this type were used, but there is no doubt about their importance in the lives of the people as the focal point of their tribal ancestor-worship and identity, for we have only to consider the enormous amount of time and energy expended on these 'non-productive' structures, at the expense perhaps of more pressing domestic tasks, to make us realise that man did not live by bread alone.

These sites were places of pilgrimage, drawing in scattered farming and hunting communities to hold vast celebrations in honour of their ancestors and to acknowledge their dependence on forces outside themselves; everything in the construction of these monuments is symbolic of what they believed.

In the last centuries of what we know as 'prehistory', the Iron Age people, sometimes controversially referred to as 'Celts', particularly venerated water. Some of what we know about these people was written down, but the accounts must be taken with a pinch of salt because they were written mainly by their enemies, particularly the Romans whose propaganda machine was anxious to justify some of their incomparable cruelties in dealing with those of whom they wanted to be rid. The Druids in particular had a hard press, but ironically their name has survived more than most other early people, as we see in the number of monuments wrongly attributed to them. Long Meg in Cumbria is still signposted today as the 'Druids' Circle', for example.

36 Image of a warrior god on a Roman shrine near Holystone, recreated in a weaving by Jane Beckensall

Early Christians were quick to realise that it was better to use existing pagan sacred places for the sites of their churches and shrines than to establish new ones, and in the sixth century, Pope Gregory the Great told Saint Augustine to build churches on pagan places of worship in England. In this pragmatic way Christianity thrived; worshippers could go on believing that little had changed, until eventually only the vestiges of paganism survived. In time, rich people began to look far afield instead of visiting local shrines, even when there were many close by to choose from – shrines became more numerous and many became wealthier. The possession of precious relics became essential for the success of a shrine, for these early days were heavy with a belief in miracles; the bones and possessions of the saintly dead were believed to hold the power to heal or to change one's fortune. But who could tell whether a bone was genuinely from a saint? There the abuse of people's faith in such relics began, but if people really believed them to hold power, perhaps miracles of a sort may have resulted from what we know as faith healing.

To be a pilgrim meant that one had to go on a journey. Pilgrims carried a 'scrip' in which to carry things or to receive offerings, and a 'bourdon'- a tall staff. Their garb made them recognisable so that people would offer help, but of course the system could be open to abuse, so they were expected to carry a letter from the parish priest or lord to acknowledge their genuine status. Some pilgrims, called *palmers*, carried palms brought from the Holy Land. They were always on the move and had no permanent home – professional pilgrims if you like – although without a doubt some would have been little more than mendicants. The idea of pilgrimage was to walk to a shrine and to pray there, a public affirmation of faith. It could be that the pilgrim had made a vow, for one of many reasons, to do the journey as a thanksgiving or as an act of penance. Shakespeare writes of King Henry IV making a vow to go to Jerusalem to do penance for his part in the murder of Richard II, but affairs of state (including a problem prince) made him leave it too late. Chaucer's fourteenth-century pilgrims were a motley crew with all sorts of reasons for going on the journey to Canterbury, one of which was that it was springtime when the senses quicken and the idea of a change and a holiday was appealing.

In the summer, pilgrims could sleep out or stay at hostelries or monasteries. Those who travelled to the Holy Land might be protected and housed by the Knights Templars and Hospitallers, who also occasionally ran hostels in Britain before the Orders were dissolved. Some pilgrimages were undertaken as 'indulgences', granted automatically if high-profile sites such as Rome, Santiago de Compostella (Iago being Spanish for James) or Canterbury were visited. Relics in these places were duplicated to an absurd degree: the scattered remnants of the 'true cross' could have rebuilt Noah's ark. There is a joke about a modern tourist being approached by a local man who offered to sell him the skull of a famous saint. He had forgotten that he had already sold one to this tourist the previous year; this skull was smaller, and the seller tried to explain that it was the same saint when he was younger! Whatever we may believe in our scientific age, in past times relics were of enormous importance to churches, and even the Venerable Bede's relics were stolen and housed in Durham, presumably by monks, who were made ruthless in this instance because authentic relics were a great prize that brought prestige to a religious foundation.

Pilgrimages had begun to decline in importance even before the Dissolution of the Monasteries; and after that, shrines were especially targeted for destruction. Many people found it highly objectionable to find Mary, who is believed to have been a poor, working-class woman, dressed up ornately and placed in some theatrical setting. Arguments against such 'idolatry' helped to fuel the ruthless iconoclasm of the Reformers, the argument being that if pilgrimage becomes theatre and industry there is the danger that it loses the purity of its intention to help people to achieve something higher and to enrich their lives spiritually.

The sanctity of shrines, however, lived on in the 'Old Faith' regions such as Holywell in north Wales, and today pilgrimages have been revived to places like Walsingham and Canterbury. In western Ireland the sacred mountain of Croagh Patrick has never lost its appeal, and today there are astonishing feats of self-abasement and physical hardship among its many pilgrims. The site is enormously powerful in its position close to the sea, visible for many miles around, and it has been found that at a special time of the year the setting sun appears to roll down its sloping side, confirmed by photographs that have arrested the progress of its movement. But pilgrimages, like everything else, have to be considered very carefully.

To understand the importance of Holy Island and of 'holy places' connected with it, we have to go back to the foundation of Christianity in Northumberland. In the process there will be some places for you to visit, many off the beaten track, but some easily accessible. Although Christianity had become the 'official' religion for a while in the later stages of the Roman Empire, the pagans who invaded Britain from Scandinavia and north Germany eliminated it here until it resurfaced in the late sixth and early seventh century. By that time groups of settlers had put down roots, giving their Old English names to the landscape, those settlers in Northumberland being 'Anglians'. By the time Edwin was king of Northumbria in the early seventh century, the kingdom was ready to take on considerable political power. He was married to Aethelburgh (Ethelburga), the sister of the first Christian king of Kent, who was granted the right to worship in her own way and who brought with her a monk called Paulinus to be her guide and to help her to convert her husband and his people. Edwin increased his earthly power by conquering Wessex, North Wales, Anglesey and the Isle of Man.

This early history was recorded by Bede of Jarrow, who drew on wide sources of information for his account of how the Church began and developed. He tells us that Edwin had called his council together at Goodmanham near York, where one of his counsellors used a striking vision of the present and the hereafter to show why the people should convert to Christianity. We are given the picture of a great hall or 'palace', into which a sparrow flies 'through the room where you sit at dinner on a winter's day with your thanes and counsellors. In the midst there is a good fire to warm the hall; outside the storms of winter rain and snow are raging. The sparrow flies swiftly in through one door, and out through another. While he is within, he is safe from the winter storms; but after a brief moment of comfort, he vanishes from sight into the dark wintry world from which he had emerged'. So wrote Bede, and the point of the image comes immediately afterwards:

> Even so man appears on earth for a while; but of what went before, or of what is to follow, we know nothing. If, therefore, this new doctrine contains something more certain, it seems only right that we should follow it.

According to Bede, the chief pagan priest was so inspired by this that he denounced his gods and rode into the temple, smashing the idols and burning the shrine.

Nowadays we do not often encounter true 'wintry darkness' out of doors, because there is so much reflected light in the sky, but there is a chance of experiencing it in the remoter parts of the Northumberland countryside. If we stand in places where these large halls may have been or were known to have been, places like Yeavering, in a valley with a winter storm raging, we can appreciate the effect of Bede's image.

Edwin was converted, his decision reinforced by the safe delivery of his baby daughter. It was a choice, and a road taken, and things would never be the same again. In AD 627 he was baptized at York, 'along with all the nobility of the nations, and a large number of the common sort'. Paulinus became Bishop of York. Conversions were so rapid and numerous that it was reported that a ceremony of baptism at Yeavering lasted 36 days.

Yeavering is now a backwater and it is easy simply to pass by the site where these great events took place, yet a lay-by on the road from Wooler to Yetholm has a gate that leads into a level field that hides an extraordinary secret, revealed, like so many others, from the air. Modern archaeologists have followed up the clues, and

37 The hills and valleys in the Yeavering area

buried ditches and the foundations of timber buildings have been revealed in this 'featureless' field. Here was one of Edwin's 'palaces', made of timber, set in a large enclosure full of other buildings. Not confined to this one field, it spills over into the fields to the south, across the road. It is also close to the River Glen, where the baptisms are supposed to have taken place. The focal point in the settlement was the Great Hall, about 25m (82ft) long and 11m (36ft) high, with aisles, and perhaps 5m (16ft) high, with a main door and side doors. It was built of wooden planks, and one imagines it to be rather like the hall that figures in the Anglo-Saxon epic poem 'Beowulf'. It was a site of rewards and punishment, with a large enclosure for the animals due as tribute to the king. It was a place of feasting and for a display of power. It is also known to have been built on the site of a pagan temple.

Today you will be greeted by a modern carved wooden wild goat's head, for the name originates as *Ad Gefrin*, meaning 'of the wild goats', and wild goats still roam the hills overlooking the site. Very recently an information board has been added.

This site is a good starting point for wider exploration of the area, for this is one of the most interesting parts of the north, its setting having great beauty and power. It was built on a glacial terrace in a valley; dominating it from the south are the rounded outcrops of the Cheviot Hills, once formed by volcanoes, with Yeavering Bell prominent. A 'bell' is a hill, and Yeavering Bell is part of a series of hills rolling south, where 'hills upon hills arise'. This hill is saddle-shaped; from its summit you can see the whole of the Milfield Plain, the Glen valley and sandstone ridges drawing the eye to the North Sea – one reward for taking paths there.

Not long ago the route was vague and you might have found yourself with a particularly tough unmarked climb, but today it has been made easier by the National Trust's way-marked paths that lead you to the summit and down again. There is a hard surface track to begin with, which leads from the road past a row of modern farm cottages and an almost-ruined barn that has the massive foundations of what might have been a bastle house, after which the turnoff takes you across fields. Approaching the Bell from the south, if you look carefully when the vegetation is fairly low, you will be able to see signs of ancient settlements and more recent temporary shelters for shepherds, and, with some luck, the wild goats. The summit has a massive wall of quarried and cobble stones enclosing a hillfort with the biggest area in Northumberland. Inside there are traces of over 130 hut circles that were probably used not only in pre-Roman times but throughout the Roman period, though the Romans had drawn their frontier line at Hadrian's Wall and tended to leave security to patrols. This high place is often cold and windy, even in summer, but judging by its size it must have been an important centre for the tribe that lived around it: the Votadini. It is clear from the Anglian settlement in the fields below that the extensive field of vision for the inhabitants or defenders was the key to their choice of place. Edwin preferred his base to be lower down, warmer and among rich farmland. Both places were a meeting place, a kind of community centre, a location perhaps where laws were enforced and trade carried out, and where people felt that they belonged to something bigger than a single farmstead.

The earlier, prehistoric people buried their dead on the hills and in the valley below had small henges, and lived out part of their lives in roundhouses, hunting in the hills, pasturing flocks and herds there, growing food and fishing in the river. The securing of food supplies and a comfortable place to live were essential at any time in history. Edwin chose this place for one of his palaces (his other base was at Bamburgh) because it was already a regional centre, and had been for centuries. It was therefore appropriate that the conversions to Christianity should take place here.

Paulinus and the Deacon James began the work of mass baptism in the River Glen. The ancient commandment to love God and one's neighbour were the core of the message. Some believers were moved to abandon everything to achieve complete communion with God – hence the monasteries with their fixed intent and their opportunity for self-denial. If we begin to understand this, we begin to understand why people like Paulinus, Aidan and Cuthbert did what they did. What about the people who were the object of their proselytising? Many were moved and were converted by inclination, but others saw only that they could do little other than to obey the wishes of their king.

Eventually the site of royal power was moved to the Milfield Plain, a rich, flat agricultural area that had been inhabited from the Middle Stone Age. Fragmentary details of life on the Plain are exposed year by year by archaeological excavation. The site of that new palace, Maelmin, after which Milfield is named, remains a shadow

38 Faint traces of the Yeavering settlement (in the foreground)

under the grass, not yet excavated in any way. It was not long after the baptism that Edwin was killed, but before we pursue the story, we will pause in this area. The most recently established St Cuthbert's Way does not actually go though Yeavering, but heads towards Wooler to the south and south-east, with access points to it from the valley. No doubt pilgrims will want to include either Kirknewton or Yeavering. Flanked by hills that are covered with prehistoric remains, Kirknewton village is a small settlement, named as a new township with a church. One reason for visiting is to see the beauty of the modern church tower, built of a variety of coloured, shaped and textured stone, and incorporating a grave slab of a little girl of the thirteenth or fourteenth century. Another is its barrel-vaulted chancel. However, my main reason for directing you there is for the piece of sculpture re-positioned on a wall inside, known as 'The Kilted Magi'.

The sandstone fragment depicts the Magi bringing gifts to Mary and Jesus; these men are seen in profile, knees slightly bent as though moving or about to kneel, each carrying a gift in one hand. They wear skirts, common in pictures at that time, but interpreted by some as kilts – hence the sobriquet. Mary and Jesus are not in profile, but face us. The work is early and difficult to date precisely, and it depicts one of the central stories of the nativity, in which other people from other lands share in the birth of Jesus – a Saviour for the Gentiles as well as for the Jews. As for the Magi, they resemble in some ways the Pictish sculptures across the Border. In this place we can see that Christianity has moved forward from the time of Edwin and Paulinus.

39 The Magi, in Kirknewton church

Outside, the gravestones show a change in the way the dead were regarded, their inscriptions and images saying a great deal about changes in fashion. Buried here is one who must have had the same missionary zeal as the early saints: Josephine Butler, who worked so hard on behalf of the abused and destitute women of Victorian England. At the gateway into the churchyard we observe the graves of young pilots killed during World War II, from different parts of the Commonwealth.

To return to Edwin: he increased contacts between his kingdom, the Continent and Rome by becoming a Christian – an important thread in the story, as the influence of Northumbria was to spread throughout Europe. However, he was killed by Mercians and Welsh people in AD 633 at Hatfield Chase, causing Paulinus and the Queen to flee, leaving James the Deacon to continue the work of conversion. Cadwalla became ruler, and it is interesting to note that he was descended from the Votadini tribe centred on Yeavering. Much of his brand of Christianity was to survive in the north, compared with the impact of Paulinus and Edwin.

Our focus now changes to that other great centre of pilgrimage, Iona. Oswald had fled and had lived with his brother in Dalriada, near Kilmartin in Argyll, for eighteen years, falling under the influence of the monks of Iona. Oswald's father had been killed by a combination of Edwin's and Redwald's armies (from East Anglia). He returned to Northumbria and killed Cadwalla at Heavenfield (the even field) near Hexham, another place favoured by pilgrims to this day, though not necessarily the actual site of the battle.

Oswald was responsible for bringing Aidan to Northumberland, one of the greatest of the early missionaries, whose success must be attributed to his personal magnetism and example. He is known as the 'Apostle of Northumbria', and was consecrated bishop at Holy Island in AD 635 within sight of Bamburgh. Oswald even acted as Aidan's interpreter on some of his missions. Here we have King and Bishop, secular and religious authority, working together with a common purpose. Aidan lived a life of poverty and travelled by foot on his missions. His brand of Christianity was different from that influenced by Rome: his church was based on small groups of people living in monastic communities, ruled by an abbot or abbess; they existed because rulers granted them the means to do so, and the abbots came from the same ruling class. His monastery on Lindisfarne would have consisted of buildings clustered around a church, all enclosed by banks and ditches. When he died he was buried on Lindisfarne.

In AD 642 Oswald was killed by the aggressive Penda of Mercia. He met his end at Old Oswestry, named after him, where his head, arms and legs were cut off and displayed. These relics were collected by his brother and enshrined in churches at Bamburgh and Lindisfarne, the body being buried in Lincolnshire. He became a 'royal saint' on account of the miracles attributed to him. After this, Northumbria was divided, but by the time Aidan died near Bamburgh in 651 he had left Lindisfarne as an established base for conversions and evangelism. He had a great influence on Saint Hilda of Whitby, who followed his example by furthering the Gospel through simple stories and songs. The story of Caedmon the herdsboy, who set the Creation story to music, is an example of such an approach. At the same time Saint Hilda's wealth was used to promote more sophisticated learning.

There is a statue of Aidan on Lindisfarne, and in Northumberland he is widely venerated, but it is perhaps Cuthbert (c.630-687) who was adopted as the pre-eminent Northumbrian saint. The pilgrimage trail today is directed in his footsteps, or rather, in the footsteps of the monks who carried his body to safety.

Cuthbert began his religious life in Melrose in AD 651, and became Prior there. He was called to serve on Lindisfarne, became Prior in AD 664, but retained his monastic detachment by travelling over to the Farne Islands in AD 676, keeping a small cell, with a plot of land and a spring. Cuthbert had charm and was a good speaker; he was persuaded by King Egfrid to become Bishop of Hexham in AD 685 while he was still on the Farnes. He was bishop for only two years, after which he resigned and returned to the Farnes, which says much about him. Cuthbert's spiritual life demanded that his cell should be isolated, with no distractions, so that his attention was directed heavenward; he needed to have completely undivided attention for God. When he died on Inner Farne in AD 687 the monks lit bonfires to signal to Lindisfarne that he had died, and his returning body was met by the entire community.

David Hall (1988 Eds. Bonner, G., Rollason & D., Stancliffe) quotes Cuthbert's prophetic warning about the dangers of removing his body from the Farnes to Holy Island:

40 A fifteenth-century painting of Cuthbert in Hexham Abbey

> I also think that it will be more expedient for you that I should remain here, on account of the influx of fugitives and guilty men of every sort, who will flee to my body because, unworthy though I am, reports about me as a servant of God have nevertheless gone forth, and you will be compelled very frequently to intercede with the powers of this world on behalf of such men, and so will be put to much trouble on account of the presence of my body.

His monks gathered round the death bed on Inner Farne and pleaded with him that they could move his body. His reply was:

> If you wish to set aside my plans and to take my body back there, it seems best that you entomb it in the interior of your church, so that while you yourselves can visit my sepulchre when you wish, it may be in your own power to decide whether any of those who come thither should approach it.

David Hall concludes:

> Those who came were pilgrims, priests, kings, murderers and felons of all kinds.

41 Cuthbert in a modern stained glass window in Beltingham

The monks washed his body, clothed him with a priest's robe and face cloth and placed the sacraments on his breast. They put sandals on his feet and then gently placed his body in a stone coffin and interred it on the right-hand side of the altar of the church. After 698 his body was transferred to a shrine and became a focus of pilgrimage. It was put into a carved wooden chest and became one of the most famous of all Anglo-Saxon shrines.

In AD 793 the Vikings arrived. Bede wrote in horror: 'The plunder of the churches exceeded their most sanguine expectations, and their route was marked by the mangled carcasses of the nuns, the monks, and the priests, whom they had massacred.' On Lindisfarne 'their impiety polluted the altars, and their rapacity was rewarded with their gold and silver ornaments, the oblations of gratitude and devotion. The monks endeavoured by concealment to elude their cruelty; but the greater number were discovered and were either slaughtered on the island or drowned in the sea'. Alcuin, formerly of York, wrote, 'The man who can think of this calamity without being struck with terror, who does not in consequence begin to amend his ways, and who does not cry to God on behalf of his country, has a heart not of flesh, but of stone.'

Imagine, then, the joy of the monks who returned to Lindisfarne after this carnage to find that Cuthbert's remains had escaped the destructive frenzy. It was decided that it was not safe enough to keep it there in a shrine in perpetuity, and in AD 875 the order was given for its removal. Bishop Eardulf decreed that Cuthbert's body should accompany the brethren into exile; the shrine was removed and people were chosen to bear the sacred remains to a place of security. It is recorded by Simeon of Durham that they took not only Cuthbert's body but the relics of some other saints: the head of Oswald, hitherto buried in the cemetery there, some of Aidan's bones, and the bones of Cuthbert's successors. These were put into a wooden coffin and it was reported that, when they were ready, a miracle happened: the sea kept back its waters, leaving a dry path to the mainland. The coffin was followed by men, women, girls and boys, herds and flocks – a veritable exodus. After they reached the mainland, the waters closed in again, with obvious echoes of the Old Testament story of the crossing of the Red Sea.

It was reported that, because the Danes still ravaged the land, the body was carried for seven years from settlement to settlement. So what route did this procession take? There are few places that they did not visit, apparently. Ancient Northumbria has many places with churches and chapels dedicated to him, such as Norham, Bedlington, Carham, Elsdon, Haydon Bridge and Beltingham. Perhaps crosses, too, were erected at places where the body rested. The hills would have been the most secure refuge after the island, perhaps beginning at the Kyloe hills and then moving towards the Cheviots. Amongst the bearers would have been Bishop Eardulf, Eadred Abbot of Carlisle, the brethren of the monastery and the laymen who chose to follow the saint.

'They wandered from place to place, throughout the whole of Northumbria, like sheep flying from wolves, and confided to the care and guidance of their leader'. Seven were chosen for the task of bearing the coffin, according to Simeon; it seems to have been carried manually at first, then in a horse-drawn or donkey-drawn cart. When there was no other shelter, tents were used. Wherever the body went it was greeted by throngs of people, some of them kneeling down, offering money or giving precious garments and silks, linen, flax, woollen cloth, fleeces, bread and cheese. We know that some of the first places visited were in the far north of today's Northumberland and in southern Scotland. They carried the precious cargo to Melrose in Scotland, remaining there for a little time, and then put the remains in a stone coffin which they sailed down to Tillmouth, presumably on a raft. Elsdon was probably one of the earliest places visited, then it might have followed the River Reed to Bellingham, following the North and South Tyne to Haydon Bridge, then on to Beltingham. Other places visited may have included Cuthbert's cave and Cuddy's cove, as their names suggest.

According to the tale, they went into Cumbria, to Bewcastle, Carlisle, Salkeld, Edenhall, Cockermouth, and so to Penrith, into Lancashire, Yorkshire, Richmondshire and Cleveland.

There is no authentic account of the places visited, but in 881 or 882 the bearers, exhausted with the responsibility, must have despaired of ever finding peace in Northumbria or even England, and were driven to make an attempt to take the body to Ireland. Again, fact and fiction are woven together. The boat sailing to Ireland was met with a great storm in which a copy of the Gospels, covered with gold and jewels, fell into the sea. It was even said that the waves turned into blood. They returned to shore near Whithorn (in modern Galloway) and begged for forgiveness. One of the men had a vision of the lost Gospels, which they retrieved, unspoiled, from a beach from which the sea had retreated further than at low tide. Some even reported that the book was even more beautiful after it had been in the sea. The horse and cart were found, harnessed, following information given by Cuthbert in a vision. They continued their journey, though they suffered fatigue, and had little to eat except a little cheese and horseflesh while they were in the land of the Picts.

At Whithorn the monks received them well, and they remained there for some time, no doubt being refreshed spiritually and physically. We hear that when they eventually arrived at Crake, north of York, in 882, they remained in the monastery for four months, then went through Darlington and Billingham, reaching Chester-le-Street in 883 and remaining there until 885 AD, after which it was taken to Durham.

The importance of St Cuthbert to Durham is highlighted by the building of the Chapel of the Nine Altars in the late thirteenth century to incorporate his remains, an addition which completely altered the eastern apse. A canopied shrine was built over the tomb, which naturally became a very important place of pilgrimage.

What, then, of the paths that lead to Holy Island? To what kind of place are they aiming? Holy Island is of prime importance to the establishment of British Christianity. Islands are special places – it takes an effort to get there by boat, and it is difficult to leave them in bad weather. They are places of solitude, an essential factor in the contemplative life. In many ways the sea protects them, although as we know, the arrival of powerful seafaring raiders such as the Vikings makes them vulnerable, too.

Even when an island like Lindisfarne was colonised as a base for the spread of the Gospel, the other Farne Islands were chosen as places to which to escape from the few people on the main island. Lindisfarne had a church and specific buildings such as cells and workshops and there would have been a refectory and guest house. Fields surrounded the settlement and lay people would have joined in the work of farming and fishing. It was a base for evangelism, the spreading of the Word throughout the land, beginning locally. It remained as such until the Viking destruction in 875, after which it was re-established by Durham Benedictine monks. The island to be known as Lindisfarne was originally *Insula Lindisfarenensis*, then *Lindisfaronensis* in 730, and *Lindisfarena ea* in 890. *Lindis* is the name for north Lincolnshire, *faran* are travellers, and *ea* is an island. Holy Island appears as *halieland* around 1150.

There is little to see now of this important monastic colony, as the site is buried under later building. The Priory is of Norman foundation, echoing the building of Durham Cathedral, being made of red sandstone with different coloured stone for its additional buildings. The parish church seems to have even older parts in its structure; there are fragments of inscribed stone that tell something of its early history, with a particularly dramatic portrayal of armed, aggressive Vikings.

The reputation of Lindisfarne is firmly established world-wide not least because of the illuminated Gospels made there. They are the work of one man above all: Eadfrith, who was bishop from 698-721. Eadfrith was the scribe, Ethelwald is reputed to have bound it; Billfrith the Anchorite added the gold, silver and jewelled ornamentation,

42 An Anglian grave slab on Holy Island, with aggressive warriors (Maureen Lazzari)

and Aldred inserted an Old English translation from the Latin. It was Simeon (or Symeon) of Durham in the early twelfth century who said that it was certainly inscribed by Eadfrith with his own hand, confirmed recently by expert examination when the modern facsimile was being prepared. Eadfrith was at Lindisfarne when the memory of Saint Cuthbert was still vivid, and shortly after Cuthbert's relics had been 'elevated'. As he was a bishop, his life must have been very hard indeed, with all the duties that it involved, so he may have completed most of his writing of the Gospels before his promotion to that office. One can imagine the faith and dedication it took to complete the task, with straining eyes, cold and often poor light.

43 A page from the facsimile of the Lindisfarne Gospels

The Word of God was of course central to doctrine, and the making of copies would make it available to more clerics, who in turn were to pass the rudiments on to the people. The Word was so revered that it was thought that only the best was good enough for its recording, transmission and preservation: thus the richly bound covers and the use of gold leaf. Only the trained and gifted could carry out this task, but it required the kind of concentration that a monastic cell or workshop would afford, along with the strength and persistence of the artist.

Bearing in mind the turbulent times of Viking invasions and so many upheavals throughout history, especially the Reformation, it is a miracle that such a fragile document has survived at all. It now lies in the British Museum, but there is a strong campaign locally that wants it brought back to the north. The problem here is that, even if it comes back as 'heritage', very few people are going to see beyond a displayed single page, whereas when the replica is on tour someone wearing gloves is able to turn the pages. The original manuscript has taken on a kind of talismanic power for some, while others are more interested in the contents in the clearest possible form, so there will remain a conflict.

Today we can cross the causeway to Holy Island, either by walking along the staked-out path across the sand or by road. Both ways are subject to the tide, and are potentially very dangerous because the tide comes in at an alarming speed. We can follow paths over the small island that take in not only the landscape where the saints would have worked, but also the routes to old lime workings: large church-like

44 The remains of Holy Island jetty

kilns below a castle perched on basalt, and the remains of a pier where boats brought in coal or carried away the lime.

There is a Gertrude Jekyll garden of 1911, a small village, an ancient parish church and a ruined priory. The island is quite flat, and its interest lies perhaps in its wide, panoramic views with their ever-changing qualities of light and weather, which may have encouraged contemplation of the infinite. To understand the world that the Saints inhabited, to see the world through their eyes, is difficult for us. Perhaps the coast by moonlight – a cold beautiful light – illuminating part of one reality and creating a reality of its own, was for them a powerful metaphor. The sky was where God 'lived', the moon his light, disturbing, mysterious, and beautiful: heaven. They could see where the waves ended, lapping, but before creeping silver-crested upon the shore they were eternal.

Our society is sceptical about miracles; we delight in rationalism and look for scientific explanations, and few of us any longer believe in the power of relics. Yet this is irrelevant when we enter the world of the Saints, in which all things were possible, because faith was their driving force. It is easier for people who live close to nature to hope for, and put their trust in, miracles when they are threatened by sudden death, by the threats of powerful people, by the day-to-day struggle to keep alive. Peace is not just the cessation of hostilities between powerful rulers, but peace of mind, peace of heart, the struggle for right relationships with neighbours and kin, and for this we and they desperately need reassurance and strength. This what the Saints passed on to us: a sense of their link with God, his power, our drawing on forces outside ourselves, yet on something always within us. In such a world miracles happened. So the men and women who walked closest to God were by nature a part of God, mentally, spiritually and even corporally because the bodies of good people even in death retained that link with another world in which their followers desperately want to believe.

I can imagine someone at that time seeing it this way:

It is not enough, standing at the sea's edge, looking at the path of moonlight over the gentle movement of waves, to think of heaven as the darkness from which the sea sprang or the place where the moon had its home. Heaven has to be demonstrated as a human possibility, by signs, by stories, by music, buildings and objects. For we are human and heaven must not be abstract. Our sense of not knowing, our sense of awe, is reassured by the world that our senses have created for us; we see in the precious objects a material wealth beyond our reach, yet for fleeting moments we are given a glimpse of the eternal, through the creations of artists and visionaries, through the work of human hearts and hands. One who measures life through the rhythm of the seasons, of daily essential tasks, has the Church calendar to observe regular breaks in routine, or even in feasting. We have the delight of entering a building rich in imagery where voices are controlled into chants that make the hair at the back of our necks bristle, that lift us beyond the now to the hereafter. Above all are the relics of those who made all this possible, perhaps now seen as bones in a gem-set casket. In our minds the saints had God-given life, they pulsated with energy. If we are sick, this helps us to improve or be cured because we believe ardently that this has the power to help us. Surrounded by those who had detached themselves for part of their lives, but whom we saw working at times like everyone else in the fields or with their nets at the sea's edge or in the river estuary, we understood the human part of them. Monks had broken away to seek a closer walk with God through discipline, prayer, and through some kind of self-annihilation. The greatest of these men may be glimpsed poring over manuscripts in the cloister or library, re-creating them with skills beyond other's reach, disappearing for a while to God knows where, and returning excitedly with new books and new ideas for the glorification of God. And we were proud, sometimes, when foreigners came with them from their visits abroad, with their particular skills, removed from our monks in so many ways; in appearance, looks and speech, yet sharing the same enthusiasm for life and the afterlife. Their greatest, most-beloved Saints did not stand always above us with heads in the clouds, but remained deeply rooted in this landscape as we are now. The moonlight on the sea may have meant the same to them as to us. The same diseases afflicted us. Our bodies need sustenance; we need friends, and need sometimes to be alone. The greatest came from our Northumbria at this time, and in them we saw something of what we ourselves might become. They interceded with God for others in this life and the next, and that was crucial.

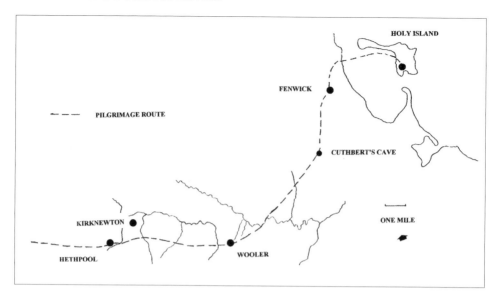

45 Cuthbert's northern pilgrimage route

ST CUTHBERT'S WAY

It is not surprising that suggested pilgrimage routes may differ from each other. There is one that starts at Hexham, but there is also an 'Official Trail Guide' published by the Stationery Office, Edinburgh (Smith, R. and Shaw, R. 1997). It is a cross-Border walk that celebrates the life of Cuthbert and it had to take into account not only places associated with him, but also that the route would cross land belonging to many different people. Fortunately, the scheme met with a rare kind of cooperation, and it takes into account the uses of the land over which it passes.

It begins at Old Melrose, where Cuthbert began his ministry, and ends at Holy Island where he died; a different concept from a route that could have begun with his death and traced the movements of his body to Chester-le-Street. However you wish to see a trail develop, this one is available, well-documented and signposted, and as the booklet and maps are in shops it would be superfluous for me to say much more. The places chosen in Northumberland begin where the route from Kirk Yetholm to Wooler passes the site very important to early Christianity at Yeavering, described above.

From Wooler the present Cuthbert trail leads across Weetwood Moor, one of the richest areas for prehistory, down the scarp to Weetwood Bridge, across to West and East Horton, from where it follows a route to the famous St Cuthbert's cave. From here Bamburgh Castle and your destination, Holy Island, become clear as you head for Fenwick. Here the route becomes very exciting for most people, along the Fishers Back Road to the Lindisfarne Causeway, spanning the tidal sands. Many choose to take the pilgrims' route across the sands themselves, marked by a line of stakes.

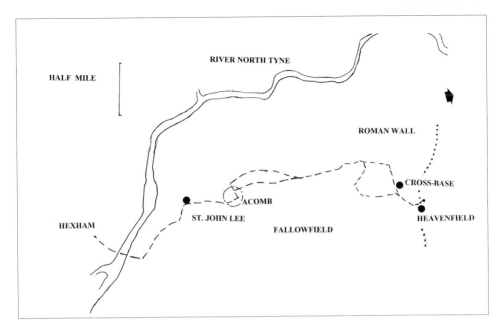

46 Oswald's Pilgrimage route from Hexham to Heavenfield

Either way, it is essential to check on the tides, otherwise you will be in danger. You are assured of superb scenery and many 'hidden' places, off the main roads.

THE OTHER ROUTE

The Roman road network continued to exist, though battered, for many years after the end of Roman rule and the arrival of the Anglians. The medieval Pilgrims' Way to Holy Island was along the Devil's Causeway (not a happy choice of name) for much of its route. The route today begins at Hexham, where beneath the Abbey the seventh-century cathedral established by Wilfrid is still partly visible in a crypt made out of stone taken from Roman forts and bridges. It makes a detour to Heavenfield, which unfortunately may not be the site of the famous battle that kept the pagans at bay, and whose name means 'the level field'. It commemorates the victor of that battle, King Oswald, later to be slain at Oswestry (literally Oswald's tree, on which his remains were displayed, and parts of which were later brought back to Northumbria as relics); thus the chapel there is St Oswald-in-Lee.

The route is well-marked and written about, passing through places such as Ryal (rye hill), Hartburn, Brinkburn, Edlingham, Whittingham, Powburn, Percy's Leap, Chillingham, St Cuthbert's Cave, Fenwick, Beal, and finally to Holy Island. All these places are of great interest, but it is impossible to deal with them all in detail here, especially as they are not actual places mentioned in the story of what happened when the body of Cuthbert was carried around northern Northumbria.

BACKGROUND THOUGHTS

When we encounter places with a story, or follow the pilgrimage routes, we may be moved by the sheer beauty of the landscape and its buildings. I prefaced my earlier book *The Power of Place* with these words:

> Places generate feelings; some do this because we have learnt what happened there, some because they are physically striking or beautiful, and others because they have some indefinable attraction and quality.
>
> When layers of time are peeled from a few special places, the result is a microcosm of the county's history. I have chosen not to present it chronologically, neither have I aimed at completeness. My responses to some places may be intellectual, based on documentary and other research, but I have included other less tangible things best expressed in poetry, when this can best describe the indescribable.
>
> Places may not affect us. We carry ourselves wherever we go, and what we see may not make much difference because we are obsessed by what is going on inside us. We may be blinkered. Unlike Byron, who says, 'I live not by myself, but become portion of that around me', we may not be open to fresh influences.

Just as we may not step into the same river twice, we may not perceive a place in the same way again. This is why it is sometimes impossible to recapture exactly what we feel when we experienced an outstanding place for the first time. Indeed, it is sometimes a mistake to revisit a place that meant a great deal at a particular time; it may have changed, and we certainly will have changed, if only a little. When we take people to see places that mean a lot to us, we may be willing them to feel what we feel, and may be disappointed if they are not affected in the same way. So, when I introduce places to you through writing and pictures, I am not asking you to feel what I feel, but am simply introducing you to the possibility that they may have value. There is nothing wrong with wanting people to share. It is the place itself that must work its own magic, if such it has.

The open country of Northumberland, especially the hills and scarplands that I find so stimulating and reassuring in a country that has become over-developed, may be unnerving to someone who has spent all his or her life in a city. It may be all right for a holiday, but not to live in. A small town with access to countryside may be the ideal place to live.

There are several problems about pilgrimage routes. There must be saints involved and they have to be authenticated. Originally they were people who had lived exemplary lives, were close to God (and therefore could act on our behalf in making our requests known to him), had done something spectacular to advance the Church, and – in the case of the early saints – their bodies had proved to be incorruptible when exhumed and their relics, either body parts, material things or even the soil

47 Holy Island from Castle to village

where they had died, had miraculous properties. People like Aidan, Bede, Hild and
Cuthbert would qualify as exceptional people in all sorts of ways, but one might
have doubts about people like Edwin and Oswald whose main claim to fame was
in the number of enemies they killed. That may be how we see it today, but in early
Anglo-Saxon times when the cult of the warrior king was uppermost, and the life
expectancy of such people was very short, pitted against strong pagan opposition,
their feats of arms made them the saviours of the Church. Without force the church
would not have survived and spread, and without the gifts of land, income and
protection, monasteries would not have flourished.

   That Oswald should have a new pilgrimage route encompassing some prime
tourist spots in Northumberland is, however, another matter. The moving of
Cuthbert's body around Northumberland to protect it and to search for a home
for it is in many ways a credible reason for a pilgrimage route, and many churches
along that route may bear his name. Oswald's great skirmish that turned the tide at
Heavenfield against invaders, and his being responsible for bringing Aidan from Iona
and for acting as his interpreter in the conversion of the local people authenticate a
route from Hexham to Heavenfield, followed by canons of Hexham Priory for many
years and still followed today by clerics and lay folk. Fragments of the cross which he
erected as a rallying point for his warriors were claimed to have miraculous powers,
and after his death at Oswestry (Oswald's tree) his body parts were scrambled for

and enshrined; his cult spread across Europe, where there are three claims to the possession of his head, as well as the one in Northumberland. Such relics gave great importance to the places where they were enshrined, and attracted pilgrims and income. Whether we should be buying Oswald T-shirts, coasters, fridge magnets or certificates of pilgrimage is doubtful, even though some of the money goes to a hospice.

People have their 'favourite' saints. One who did much to build splendid churches at Ripon, York, and Hexham and to convert Sussex was Wilfrid, but Bede, although writing in praise of his contribution to the furtherance of the Church, especially in his championing of the Roman version over the Celtic at the Synod of Whitby, does not appear to have any warmth for the man. He was a formidable friend and enemy, very talented, mixed with the aristocrats of his time, matching them in status, went to Rome when it was necessary to gather more relics and ornaments for his churches or to plead his case in a dispute to the Pope, made enemies, usually came out on top. It is so difficult to realise that to go to Rome, as many of these people did, was very arduous and hazardous; these early churchmen were made of stern stuff! We remember that when we board our transport. Bede himself lived in a monastery that was practically wiped out by plague, yet Jarrow continued to be one of the greatest sources of research and for the storing and production of sacred texts in the world. This is commitment; this is inspiration; this is heroism. Being saintly though does not mean being faultless, and, although we have our love of some, lingering dislike of others, and uncertainty about what to think, we have to be careful in our judgements.

The tracks that we take in 'the footsteps of the saints' can be a journey of self-discovery, spurred on by the fame and deeds of good people who have contributed something of great value to our culture and heritage. We may make it the road of self-discovery, to give thanks, to intercede for someone, to seek help for a problem, to look inside ourselves. We may find the act of walking along with others reassuring, strengthening faith, getting a new perspective on life as the physical effort of walking in exciting places adds to the experience. If the experience makes us more charitable, so that we give freely where we have freely received, that is all to the good. 'Go forth into the world in peace, be of good courage, hold fast that which is good, render unto no man evil for evil, strengthen the faint-hearted, support the weak, help the afflicted, honour all people' is a worthy outcome, whatever your beliefs.

4

SEASCAPES

The search for more 'out of the way places' may be extended southwards down the coastline from where Saint Cuthbert lived. Northumberland has an enormously long stretch of coastline bordering the North Sea, from which I shall choose some more special places.

RUMBLING KERN

The Northumberland coast is made up largely of sedimentary rocks; they look in many ways like the depositions left by the sea today, that have petrified. There are ripple marks left by ancient tides, and there are fossils of marine creatures embedded in limestone and of ferns and trees in sandstone. These are particularly evident in coal workings. Sometimes, as at Bamburgh, usually thought of only for its long stretch of beautiful sand, there is an outcrop of limestone with natural cracks that gives the impression that someone has laid a pavement.

Here and there are fire-formed rocks, whinstone, also called dolerite and basalt, that have oozed out over the sedimentary rocks, cooled rapidly, crystallised, and now stand in columns in contrast to the underlying near-horizontal strata. Dark in colour, ranging from deep green to black, sometimes tinted with iron, they are known as Dykes – walls of stone. Bamburgh Castle is built on them; the Farne Islands are columns, partly drowned.

At Craster, whinstone is clearly visible not only in the quarries that now house a car park, but also in the dark stones of the cottages, giving a distinctive mottled appearance. Further south, when the whinstone disappears for a while, the coast is made up of tilted layers of sandstone, limestone, shale and some coal.

Our destination here is called Rumbling Kern or Churn, named either from the rocks ('carrs') or the water churning round, and it has both: a hollow, a chasm, through which the sea pounds when the tide comes in, intensified by storms, reaching a crescendo with an almighty roar. A great spout of water reaches for the sky and

48 Limestone pavement south of Bamburgh, with the Farnes beyond

49 Bamburgh Castle, the site of modern excavations

50 Howick Bay, looking north

cascades onto the waiting rocks. This is the urgent power of the North Sea working away, as it has done for thousands of years, on a tilted coast that is gradually sinking, exposing new layers as it does so, gradually or dramatically.

My family and I used to come here frequently in the summer when we lived at Felton, often with our visitors and their children; it is a wonderful place for all ages. Some of the natural stone has been quarried away on the landward side, leaving an undisturbed low cliff between us and the sea and a small stretch of sheltered sand. This un-quarried seaward-facing ridge has a display of different bedding planes, contrasts in colour and texture, and the occasional fossilised tree bark exposed. Deposition is not a regular thing, so we see criss-crossing lines of harder sandstone, more resistant to the power of the sea, and iron-staining from natural minerals caught up in the rock layers. It forms a kaleidoscope of colour that took millions of years to establish.

One vertical quarried face has been once again attacked by the sea rushing in to fill a void, leaving a blow-hole at the base of which are the small stones that have acted like a drill when the sea moves them in a circle. This little haven is on a coastal path between Craster and Boulmer. Dunstanburgh Castle with its fortifications like fingers clutching at the sky, lies to the north. A house at the sea's edge on a small cliff, built as an up-market bathing hut, bears evidence of the power of erosion, its sandstone building-blocks etched and holed, smoothed and crumbled. We see the same pattern in the drum towers of the main gateway at Dunstanburgh Castle and the pillars of the Holy Island priory. Weaknesses in stone are found and tested by wind, frost, sea-spray and rain.

51 Rumbling Kern

52-5 (above and opposite) Four images of the rock formations

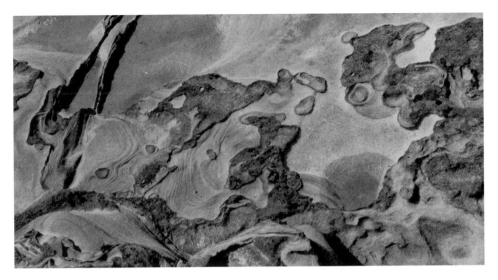

56 Rumbling Kern from the air

South of Rumbling Kern the great stretches of sand that have been interrupted by rock, especially dolerite, take over the beaches again in fine sweeps, sometimes silver, orange and brown, in places white under the sea, turning it turquoise, like the Mediterranean.

Sandstone is particularly prone to dramatic sculpting, as we see in other places in the county. Coal makes a spasmodic appearance here, only in shale seams, whereas much further down the coast are the deeply buried deposits that were the base of the Industrial Revolution. Among the layers are trilobite tails from a sea creature that resembles the modern woodlouse in some ways, seen on the coast just south of Craster. All these layers are visible in cross-section when you leave the path and go down to the rocky or sandy beaches.

River estuaries and bays are particularly important to seafarers who wish to access the hinterland. The sea is a great and constant source of food, with its abundant crustaceans, fish and kelp, a good reason why people chose to live close to the sea, especially in winter; in warmer times they could move further inland to fields or to gather wild fruits, nuts and berries or to hunt there. Not far away from Rumbling Kern, high on a cliff that has partly slipped into the sea, some of the earliest Northumbrians made their home for at least 200 years, living for some of the time in a circular hut with a thatched roof that sheltered them about 7000 years ago.

57 The coast south from Rumbling Kern

This is one of the earliest roundhouses ever discovered in Britain and it has been excavated to such a profound extent that it has changed our views about the nature of the life of these early people. It was thought that they lived in tents and other shelters, which may be true for most of the year as they pursued a mobile way of life, but here at the coast they had a more permanent home. It has long been acknowledged that people would have returned to the coast in winter, but here is proof positive. Among the remains of food around their fires were hazel nuts – an important part of their diet. Their basic raw material for tools and weapons was flint, finds of which led to the discovery of this site; they were poking out of the ground at the cliff's edge. The rest of the coast has seen similar discoveries of the tiny blades which characterise these Mesolithic (Middle Stone Age) people, who lived there before the land bridge between England and the Continent had been sunk, so that people could have walked across what is now the Channel. Sites like this prove that the sea has changed its level, as it continues to do, but at an accelerating rate because of the way we are destroying the ozone layer and causing global warming.

The traces of these early people are confined mainly to the most durable of the materials that they used, so that chippings, tiny flint barbs and arrow points are how we know of their existence. They lived in small groups for thousands of years, until the coming of arable farming and the selection of animals for breeding led to an expansion in population and more fixed places for houses and fields. So along the coasts, as well as in some inland

58 The Mesolithic house site being excavated

59 The Mesolithic hut reconstruction at Milfield

areas close to rivers, we can trace them, in the flint tools and chippings often found through things as simple as rabbit holes and mole hills, or protruding from sand banks.

History is about people, about how they came to terms with what was around them, making use of it, and at that very early period life expectation was low and the living precarious. When the search for food and shelter became less of a full-time job, presumably there was time to explore in more detail what lay beyond their own boundaries. We read and hear much today about the conflict between Darwinists and Creationists, but from a deep study of the past I am with Darwin in finding it impossible to believe in anything other than that life evolved over millions of years, a struggle leading to the survival only of those best able to adapt to changing conditions. It is this consideration that makes me so uneasy about the idea of a beneficent Creator.

When I think back to the extended family that set up their fragile home here on the Howick cliff-top, I am aware that they were at the mercy of these laws, and had no choice in the matter. If they did not hunt and gather whatever was available, they would die. Had I lived then, I too would have killed to survive, whether it were to gather seafood or to eat the flesh of animals. Creation's laws have given us no choice.

On the same site as that house a number of Early Bronze Age cists, small chests made of stone slabs for the burial of the dead, were excavated. These were deliberately placed on the cliff top and may have been covered with stone cobbles to make the burial site more visible, thousands of years after their predecessors made their little settlement here. It adds to the place another element: the importance of respecting the dead, and of choosing a place for this ceremony that would have such lovely views.

Close by too, are other signs of prehistoric life, this time in the Iron Age or Roman period, where a low-profile enclosure must have been a centre for life about 2000 years ago. Like the rocks on the beach below, we are seeing time in layers here.

As William Golding has explored in his work, a question of guilt arises when we are conscious of the choices that we are offered. The innocent have no choice in the way they are directed to survive, as was the case of the early people on the cliff top, and many who followed them were in the same position.

When we consider our human condition, we may be conscious, as Wordsworth was, of an unease and a sense of loss, or what others may have seen as 'the hopeless ache of the unobtainable'. He voices it in this way:

The Rainbow comes and goes,
And lovely is the Rose,
The Moon doth with delight
Look round her when the heavens are bare,
Waters on a starry night are beautiful and fair;
The sunshine is a glorious birth;
But yet I know, where'er I go,
That there hath past away a glory from the earth.

(From: *Ode: Intimations of Immortality* by W. Wordsworth)

60a & b Two Early Bronze Age cists: Howick and Harehope

'The meanest flower that blows' might give Wordsworth 'thoughts that do lie too deep for tears' but he did ignore the perpetual warfare going on around it. He was, though, aware of something wrong, of something missing, that we have lost the 'glory and the freshness of a dream' and lost sight of that immortal shore from which we came. His consolation was:

> Though nothing can bring back the hour
> Of splendour in the grass, of glory in the flower
> We will grieve not, rather find
> Strength in what remains behind;

This is the only hope when we face imponderable questions about creation. Whether we see this as happening millions of years ago or only 4000 years ago, as a random process or as a grand design, is in my view irrelevant when faced with the question, 'Why was it arranged like this?'

Let us then return to the grandeur of the scene, this seascape, the surge of water, forming white ripples as it ebbs and flows, the roar of water in a storm, a constant assault on soft rocks, the insistent shaping and reshaping that ensures that nothing remains exactly the same. Part of the Mesolithic settlement, this pinpoint in time, collapsed into the sea not very long ago. Our contribution to global warming has accelerated this process of the rise in sea levels and other aspects of climate change. Creation is finely balanced. There is a great gap between us and the extended family that used their cliff-top settlement as a base for survival; not only in time, but in the way we have exploited the land whilst they left it as they found it, more or less. There are millions more of us and we have developed technology to such an extent that we can literally move mountains if we wish. We have tapped enormous power sources without satisfying our need to exploit further. The more we have, the more we want, and the economic system, impelled more by multi-national companies than by governments, has created for the world an unprecedented and dangerous situation.

DRURIDGE BAY

People fight back wherever they can at a local level, and a good example of this is seen further south along this coast, where not only did open-cast mining become important but also the moving of tonnes of sand for building. Although deep mining has apparently had its day, the spoils are still with us along the coast, but they will be absorbed in the greater power of water, which after all covers about 90 per cent of the Earth's surface. Wordsworth was conscious of the way in which man was over-exploiting the land in pursuit of wealth, at the outset of the Industrial Revolution:

> The world is too much with us; late and soon,
> Getting and spending, we lay waste our powers;

Little we see in nature that is ours.
We have given our hearts away, a sordid boon!

It is natural for people to use whatever is around them to make a living, to exist, and perhaps to enjoy the luxury that a surplus can bring. But the level of exploitation, the level of inequality created by it, and the almost obscene lengths to which people will go to acquire and spend money has reached a worrying level. Not many years ago there was concern about something that at first seemed quite natural and simple. The building industry needed sand, and there was a whole stretch of it, easy to lift. Why not?

Druridge means the dry ridge, and this is composed of sand dunes. It lies next to land that has been exploited for coal, especially open-cast extraction, so there was already a tradition of industrial use. Many sites had been filled in and re-landscaped, so did it really matter if sand was taken too? Well, so many people thought that it did that it became the subject of a large public protest. And there was a more sinister threat: this part of Northumberland was also being considered as a dumping ground for nuclear waste. Protesters felt that Northumberland had already had its share of industrial exploitation, and there was a growing feeling that the vast majority of people, living in towns, were regarding it as a convenience for their leisure activities or as a source of energy, a suspicion heightened by proposals for wind farms. It also emphasised some of the traditional Tory–Labour divisions between town and country that are so dangerous. At Druridge these divisions did not count; part of a Northumberland beach was being taken away, and such beaches

61 Druridge Bay

are valued by all classes of people. No one would have considered Bamburgh or Holy Island for such use, but the tradition of mineral exploitation here meant that at first it made less impact on the public. In time, the idea that this coast was in danger of becoming an industrial wasteland took root, and artists and writers of all kinds rallied to defend it. Many would never have thought of taking the track to this place, or even knew it existed. It was a good example of everyone having their say in their future, and they won the battle. Sand extraction was stopped and the burial of nuclear waste was not mentioned again.

At the time I too was moved to consider the value of this place, and added my own poem to the large number in circulation:

DRURIDGE

Earth is a dry ridge, sediment of seas,
A breaker's yard of shell and bone and clay
Transformed to sun-soaked hollows,
Rippling light and shadow dance
Where flowers' heads splash colour on the strand.

Once we could only ruffle surfaces
In exploitation of this land.
Now we can move mountains.

Water rolls upon itself;
The sea sheds skins of waste,
Dead, ready to be transformed into another life.
Our future once was traced in scrolls of light,
Or silver streaks that ran in silence to the moon,
Where mystics linked the sea to sky.

Air poses thunder-threat from alabaster clouds,
Mingles with gull-screech, blue-torn passages of jets.
Wind skims dry sand sharply to the sea.

A caterpillar tread and hungry iron jaws
Tear and flatten in a day, carry sand away.
The menace of a glowing core, power of suns,
A self-perpetuating raging **fire** becomes
A nightmare of split atoms, nightmare of a new creation.
Nature made in us four elements;
Each part of earth, air, water, fire,
Held to be for centuries the cause of all our moods and life,
A link with laws that teach us all to have aspiring minds.
Now we are called upon to use these talents to protect the earth.

62 The dunes at Druridge

There is another problem here that no triumphant saving in one part of the country will make disappear: the 'not in my back yard' argument poses the question: where, then? It is much easier to object than to offer viable alternatives. The North East has already been vastly exploited for its mineral wealth, as we can see everywhere, but this industrial past has changed from mining, heavy industry and manufacturing to light industries, such as electronics, and to extensive retailing, most manifest at the Metro Centre, Gateshead. The legacy is all around us; although many industrial sites have been destroyed, the evidence of hundreds of others remain for us to see, despite nature's ability to cover them over: old railway tracks, bridges, mine shafts, limekilns, lead smelters, flues and chimneys – and so much more.

Newbiggin-by-the-Sea was once a great holiday resort for Victorian and later populations of Tyneside. At the heart of an industrial landscape that has been constantly modified, it has a history going back to the Mesolithic period, just like that at Howick further north. The church is placed, as were so many early churches, on a headland within easy reach of the sea, and has a graveyard with memorials that range from simple crosses to black slabs with images of footballs, cars or golfing motifs, recording the interests of the dead. The graves lead up to a wall behind which is a caravan park. Sand has now been brought in to reconstruct the beach!

Nothing seems to stay the same except the sea and the tides, although exploitation has even changed the sea in that commercial fishing has reduced fish stocks to such

63 Newbiggin

64 Newbiggin church

low levels that fishermen can no longer earn a living: all so different from the past centuries when people found it an invaluable resource. It is another reminder of where thoughtlessness and greed are leading us. We have travelled too far along that track.

5

THE BEAUTY AND SADNESS OF DESERTION

Broken-down and decaying buildings have often been a focus of romantic imagination, so much so that people have built them as 'follies'. The Gothic taste for ivy-covered ruins of priories and castles, the legends attached to them, the search by the morbid for gory details, the obsession that some people have with the spirit world, has ensured that when the normal life has gone out of a place it will be re-populated with ghosts and memories. Reaction to these old buildings is often the result of our wishing them to be a mystery, a haunting, a thrill of fear.

Jane Austen's *Northanger Abbey* is a delightful commentary on the difference between the expectations that readers of Gothic novels have of old buildings and the reality of an old abbey converted into a modern house.

There are many deserted, crumbling farm houses on the Northumberland moors and abundant derelict industrial buildings that have the power to make us think about the past and its impermanence, to speculate on who lived there and why the buildings were abandoned. They speak of changes that have taken place in economics, in the way we choose, or do not choose, to live. Norfolk has many beautiful churches with no people to attend them, the result of arable land being turned over to pasture and to the inevitable job losses that occur when machinery takes over what used to be an intensive-labour economy. In Northumberland the process of change and abandonment can be recorded in very ancient landscapes from Neolithic times onwards, when climate change, soil erosion and shifting economic forces have determined that people will no longer live in these places and be compelled to move with their families elsewhere to make a living. 'Elsewhere' has forced many to move abroad. The process is not only evident in such enterprises as the hugely important mining and smelting of lead, but also abandoned branch lines of railways, stations, limekilns and even ports such as Alnmouth. On Holy Island limekilns like churches with gothic arches are preserved but no longer used, and those at Seahouses have alternative uses. On Holy Island there are the remains of a jetty where coal used to be imported and lime exported, now looking like some abandoned prehistoric timber circle at the sea's edge.

65 Holy Island nineteenth-century limekilns from the castle

There is the overgrown waggonway curving round the coast that once brought wagon-loads of lime to the kilns. The whole of that headland, dominated by the castle on outcrops of whinstone, has been sculpted for many uses. Redundant industrial enterprises are sometimes bulldozed almost out of existence, but scars are always left.

A little-known industry is surprisingly at Brinkburn, known mainly for its beautifully situated Priory and house on the banks of the River Coquet. Most people know nothing of its existence, yet here was a Victorian enterprise that extracted coal, limestone and iron nodules from fields to the north, brought them by waggonway to a place near the Priory, and constructed small blast-furnaces to smelt them. There was even a small railway station some distance away. Now, a grass-covered circular furnace base and another with a pile of iron-rich slag remain where the operation came to a halt; the furnace split and was not repaired.

A more subtle survival may be seen in an agricultural landscape, where lynchets, terraces and rig and furrow, so common throughout Northumberland are best seen when the sun is low in the sky; showing the features as deep shadows, they trace a change in land-use. Northumberland has always been primarily agricultural, despite outbursts of other industries. The vast open spaces of the Cheviot Hills and extensive moorland elsewhere have few people living there now, yet everywhere are the signs waiting to be read of people living there: fields, farmsteads, walls and enclosures covering thousands of years of use of the land. Seen from the air, the patterns are

66 Abandoned lead-mining works at Carrshield/Coalcleugh

visible in the right light or crop conditions, but the details of who farmed them and how they lived come from archaeology.

Museums display some of these artefacts; families retain old photographs and other memoralibilia of a more recent past. It is surprising how much there is to see. At Rothbury Middle School my staff and I arranged for the whole school to spend time finding out about Cragside house, encouraging parents and children to visit it during the holiday period and to bring into school as many items as possible relating to the past.

This purpose-built house, now owned by the National Trust, is the result of one man's ambition and acumen, for Lord Armstrong was one of the great industrialists and engineers to emerge in the nineteenth century to make Britain a leading industrial nation. Having made his money through his inventive genius, he invested part of it in building a house to suit his tastes on the side of a moorland crag. He transformed the landscape by damming the streams to make lakes at different levels to provide water and height for his hydraulics, powering machines and generating electricity. Miles of paths, tracks and roads, thousands of trees and plants are his legacy and, of course, a house that drew on many different historical styles and devices that were to impress his visitors, including royalty and overseas notables. This is hardly a 'hidden' place, but it does have great scope for the exploration of its grounds, where all kinds of discoveries, such as the course of the twisted copper cables that led from generators

67 Track to Old Bewick Moor

and batteries to the house, to make a ring circuit, pass unobtrusively in their wooded troughs through the landscaped site.

This is only one part of the story; history tends to be about the famous, but they only achieve what they do through the work of others. So, there was a huge force of workers to construct and landscape, people to maintain the estate and work at 'the big house', and those who lived nearby pursuing their own lives. Everyone would be touched by the presence of Cragside, and the pupils at the school were to bring in evidence of this and of the larger picture of life in the area at that time. Furniture, greetings cards, photographs, clothes, tools, jewellery filled the classrooms. For everyone, this became a detailed and exciting picture of an age, and showed how much life has changed since then. No one had to be told that 'history matters'. Of course it does.

Whereas Cragside is preserved, as many important houses are, there are others that are much smaller and considered of less significance that cast their spell. We have seen the deserted inn at Newmoor crossroads, but there are many deserted buildings where once people who worked on the land lived. I have written elsewhere about one of the most powerful of these abandoned buildings – Blawearie – for here the atmosphere is unique in my experience. Simply as a deserted house in the middle of unpopulated moorland, with a long track leading to it from the village of Old Bewick, it is visually stunning.

Surrounded by trees that were planted in the mid-1800s in a garden cut out of solid rock, with steps and small walls, the simple two-up and two-down house-site chosen is in a landscape rich in prehistory. Its recent history includes its uses by the army as a training area during the last war, but before that it was home to the Rogerson family, shepherds who brought up a large family there. Some of the descendants have been researching their ancestors, and have recovered some very interesting photographs of Blawearie. I offer some of these photographs, with their permission.

Life there must have been hard in many ways – quite a different matter from making a casual visit today. We have only to look for the spring of water emptying into a stone trough below the house, or the 'netty' outside the house to appreciate some of the difficulties of living there, yet the children were always at school in the village, no matter what the weather, unless it was closed when the weather became too bad. It had started life possibly as the dream of one man from Eglingham who must have welcomed the solitude and beauty that it would bring to him, yet we know nothing of this man. There is nothing grandiose about the house itself, but its setting among quarried stone, utilising the stone already there makes it special. The rock outcrops, like so many other Fell sandstones, have twisted bedding-planes and look out over a deep valley of the Harehope Burn over a large spill of huge boulders detached in geological time from the outcrop.

By planting trees he was reversing what normally makes land 'waste', and he shows us what the possibilities were for a different kind of landscape hundreds of years ago. When we excavated a nearby cairn, we had the buried soil analysed, and this showed that 4000 years ago there was a covering of light woodland, where now it is mainly heather and bracken. Even after thousands of years, it is possible to encourage some landscapes to grow plants again which have disappeared. All the trees seen in the pictures were planted about 150 years ago, where there were none before.

Today shepherds or other farm-workers do not want to live in such isolation; they have transport, and they can easily cover the moors in their modern vehicles. Their children especially demand to be nearer 'civilization', the world of shops, companionship and popular music. Whereas in the past people had little and had to 'make do' with what they had, consumerism and available cash have changed all this. It is certainly a more wasteful society in which the world's resources are being consumed at an enormous rate, in which the gap between the rich and the poor is widening every day. Whether we are 'happier' now than those families who lived in places like Blawearie we cannot know, as every age has a mixture of happy and sad times, of love and hate, of security and insecurity. The population of the countryside continues to shrink, and one test of the health of a village is how many children there are. The closure of so many small village schools is an answer. Meanwhile many regard the countryside as a place of recreation, not for work, and we neglect our agriculture at our peril. One crisis in world trade which affects our food supplies, and we would soon realise the stupidity of neglecting a vital commodity. The countryside dies when young people leave it, and no wonder, when they cannot possibly compete in the housing market. The 'good life' of rural areas has become the province of the elderly and of those with 'Chelsea

68a & *b* Blawearie house and some of the Rogerson family who lived there

chariots' to speed them from place to place. Others need desperately to escape the big cities. The only good side of this is that they renovate old properties and thus save them from extinction. Blawearie is a symbol of the abandoned, yet to have it renovated and made inaccessible to us would be even sadder.

There are many tracks leading to and from Blawearie house. Some of them, grassed over now, are hollow ways made either by the transporting of stone from

69 The Rogerson family at Blawearie

70 Blawearie house

1 Alemouth Corn Road at Hexham: now cut off by a new road

2 Thockrington church

3 Debdon Whitefield moor

4 The old stagecoach road, Rimside

5 Caller Crag

6 Corby's Crag top

7 A disused bell pit – one of many

8 Hareshaw Linn, Bellingham

9 Hareshaw Linn bridge

10 The Ingram valley

11 Cheviot landscape from Brough Law to Linhope

12 Linhope Spout edge

13 Linhope Spout from the south

14 Roughting Linn

15 Whinstone and Holy Island Castle

16 Howick coast formations

17 Blawearie

18 Blawearie excavated cairns

19 Fowberry cairn going back to nature (autumn, 2008)

20 Hartburn grotto

21 The Salters' Way at Shaftoe

22 A Mesolithic rock-shelter at Shaftoe Crags

23 Shaftoe Crags hidden in woodland

24 The Hopper Mausoleum, Whittonstall

25 A superb revelation: rock art at Ketley Crag (© Brian Kerr)

71 Almost uninhabited country: Ros Castle

quarries or the result of military exercises during the Second World War. The track up to Blawearie from the village was resurfaced by Italian prisoners of war, who were housed locally. All these and others are seen clearly from the air, and there are other routes that are now footpaths.

Blawearie is a base for exciting exploration; there are faint tracks heading north over Hepburn Moor, where prehistoric burial mounds show that the name was well-chosen, for it means the high burial mounds. From the scarp you look right across the River Breamish/Till valley to the Cheviot Hills, and below you is Blawearie house. As you walk north, with the hill called Ros Castle always in sight to the north-east, there is the planted forest of Hepburn Wood to the east below the scarp, and a prehistoric enclosure from which, again, there is an extensive view to the hills and over Chillingham Park, with its castle, tower and wild cattle. This track reaches a minor road below Ros Castle, which is a dominant hill, visible for miles around, with a prehistoric defensive enclosure on top. The name means a fortification on either a hill or moor, depending whether it comes form the Irish *ros* or the Welsh *rhos*. From here, after the climb to the summit, your reward is one of the most widespread views of moorland sweeping towards the North Sea, which ends roughly on the route of the modern A1 road.

From here you have almost unlimited choice of which paths to follow, but I will return you to the minor road. Wherever we walk, we will be struck by the lack of human habitation, yet this was an area where prehistoric people thrived. Much has been planted with trees, and there are patches of bog among coarse grasses and mosses. It is as well to keep to the trackways, although these too can turn out to be boggy. I have spent

72 The Harehope valley

many hours off the beaten tracks exploring this landscape, and it can be a physically demanding and wet experience. On Quarry House Moor there is a marked track off the road, back to Blawearie to the right of the Harehope valley, a valley for which it is well worth leaving the beaten track to see lovely rock formations and overhangs, with a scattering of rowan trees in the sheltered places along the narrow valley floor.

It does not matter which way you turn; there are interests and delights everywhere. You could turn off the Blawearie track to stand high above the burn at Corbie Crags (yet another crag named after crows) and look at the landscape from a perched block on a scarp edge.

You will find it difficult to believe that you are in an over-populated country. Again, there is the insistent reminder that this landscape provided homes and a living for people for centuries. Above the Harehope Burn is an Iron Age enclosure, and on the Old Bewick scarp is a large, unique spectacle-shaped hillfort.

There are many explanations for the changes in population and for the building and desertion of homes. One is that the fertility of the land has changed, as temperature has changed over the thousands of years, for the soil must always have been thin. Quarries for sand and limestone abound, but there are almost no remaining outlines of fields, so it is possible that we are looking at a landscape that has always been mostly open and unfenced.

73 Harehope: a perched boulder

Market forces, in so many ways a curse to stable societies, have always dictated where people should live. There have been many small industries scattered across Northumberland because raw materials such as coal, lead, iron, lime and stone have been available. The Pennine region has a particular concentration of abandoned industries and houses. It is not strictly true to classify these places as a 'wilderness', or a place of 'outstanding natural beauty', because its landscape has been changed by industrial operations. Lead ore was extracted either through 'hushing' (building up a head of water above a valley then letting it wash the galena-bearing rock formations clean) or by digging into the ground, all signs still abundantly visible. There were places where the ore was broken up and washed, places where the ore was smelted, leaving flue tunnels to run across the country until they reached tall chimneys to take way the lethal fumes.

Although coal was mined mainly on the coast, there were many smaller mines inland, now mostly abandoned. One of the most interesting, and again off the beaten track, is at Ford Moss, away from the castle and village or the attractions of Heatherslaw Mill and Etal Castle. Here you may enter another world, where nature has reclaimed a whole coalmining community, with terraced house foundations still visible, a chimney that was part of the mechanism of raising and lowering pitmen into the mine, an engine shed, a waggonway, early bell-pits, an associated quarry and much more. The railway failed to reach it, and that made transport here uncompetitive, a factor that helped to end centuries of mining, so today the mole hills and rabbit holes throw up fragments of people's lives: pottery, bits of ironwork and

74 Old Bewick hillfort; a recent collapse shows how one wall was built

75 South of the Hexham–Alston road

76 Ford Moss abandoned coalfield

even parts of a doll, while the rhubarb planted in the gardens or planted daffodils reappear very year, but with no one to enjoy them.

The mining areas were not often reached by the established church, but Methodists and other Nonconformists filled the spiritual gap, leaving a legacy of chapels everywhere, now converted to private houses. It is another aspect of desertion.

Abandoned buildings become a fair target for builders; most of the Roman Wall and its buildings was eventually recycled. The rubbish of yesterday becomes the archaeology of today.

What happened to buildings when industries closed down? Some houses were left, simply to fall down on their own. The lead-workers favoured small crofts where they could keep a cow and grow vegetables and a little fruit, so these houses had walled gardens that became overgrown. Abandoned houses are sources of roof slabs and stone, and once the stripping begins the collapse is rapid. What is left is a life lost, where before each house had children and adults, love, tribulation, joy, sadness, arguments, aspirations. Does anything linger on, or do we imagine all these things when we see an isolated, abandoned home? To see a building from which its purpose has been taken is disconcerting and painful. When I was a small boy, the sight of two swimming pools in Stoke-on-Trent that had been cracked and emptied by mining subsidence made me afraid, and the sight of an empty pool is still something that makes me feel very uneasy. As one who loved to swim, deep water had no terrors for me, but the empty swimming pool had. The crack along the base tiles was like W.H. Auden's 'lane to the land of the dead':

The glacier knocks in the cupboard,
The desert sighs in the bed.
And the crack in the tea-cup opens
The lane to the land of the dead.'
(From 'As I walked out one evening')

Perhaps these experiences give form to our inner emptiness, something that we all fear, that hollow in the stomach when we do not know why we are so apprehensive, the unprovoked panic, what E.M. Forster bases *Howard's End* on: 'panic and emptiness'. For some of us, abandonment of what gave life to so many may become a metaphor for all that is uncertain in life.

Abandonment on a big scale occurs when whole villages disappear, usually because their populations are no longer required for work on the land or in other industries, and rarely because they have been destroyed by disease. We saw what happened to Thockrington, but what happened at Ancroft was on a much larger scale, when Plague struck. Plague was so horrendous that at its height (The Black Death) it almost halved the population of Britain. Ancroft is but one example. The village today lies on the road from Ford to Berwick-on-Tweed. The major surviving old building is a church, but on the corner of the road is a field where no one is allowed to build, where in low light all the plots of land, house sites and lanes are visible as mounds and ditches. Overlooking it is a long row of trees, reputedly planted to represent the families that died of disease. Their bodies were taken away from the site further east, where they were cremated. The church of St Anne (which is not, however the origin of the place name, which means a lonely or isolated croft) is partly Norman, including a blocked doorway on the south, which meets you as you approach from the small parking space. The photograph shows what an attractive feature this is in its setting.

A century later a tunnel-vaulted tower of great strength was added, reached by an inner spiral staircase leading to an upper room where the vicar might have lived. The church was considerably restored and extended in the nineteenth century.

In the churchyard is an interesting grave stone which commemorates nuns who had fled from France during the 1789 Revolution and found sanctuary at Haggerston Castle.

The two episodes here commemorating death by disease and the perils of living in a country in chaos, find a place in this quiet little settlement.

A final example from so many is at South Middleton, near Hartburn and Shaftoe crags. The air photograph shows the site of a village, with house foundations, gardens attached to each one, running east to west, roads and the surrounding typical 'rig and furrow' farming, some of which overlies the village plots and is therefore later than them. Twelve people were tax payers in 1296, and there were still four cottages in use as late as 1635. It is like so many others in England that have been made particularly well known by a series of excavations that explored how these villages functioned and why they vanished. Clearly this village did not vanish completely.

Above 77 Ancroft church, next to an abandoned village

Right 78 The deserted village of South Middleton (Newcastle University)

John Hodgson, renowned local historian and vicar of Hartburn in the nineteenth century, writes this:

> In the inquest after the death of Roger Fenwick, in 1635, South Middleton is described as a ville consisting of 8 messuages, 4 cottages, 130 acres of arable land, 60 of meadow, 150 of whin and heath, and as having common pasture for all cattle in it and in Corridge.

The township probably had what are now North Middleton, Corridge, and Highlaws within it. The present farm is actually half a mile south of the old village site.

Nearby is the little village of Hartburn. It is reached by a road running from the south that cuts the Middleton village in half, so look out for what is on either side of you.

With Shaftoe and the deserted village of South Middleton nearby, Hartburn is most worthy to be included as a place to visit. The land on which its church is built and the plots of its ancient village lies between two streams, the larger being the Hart Burn, towards which the land drops steeply away on the north side. The road to Scots Gap has a number of modern, well-built and spacious houses built as a minor ribbon development, behind some of which lies a fascinating woodland walk above and leading down to the stream bank. The narrow paths are not overdone – just a little help given with wooden footbridges or the shoring up of paths on a slope. Signposted and welcoming, the two entrances to the walk stand at either end of a circuit that takes in the gorge-like quality of this valley and its fast-flowing water, in places cutting through sandstone to form cliffs, and widening out where its old course and melting ice would have run. The constant rush of water, the surprise of the views encountered and the abundant plant and animal life are reasons enough to enjoy this place, but it has an additional special distinction: a grotto.

The name associated with this and with the development of the Glebe lands in particular is Dr Sharpe, who was vicar of Hartburn from 1749-92. He lived at a time when 'follies' were in vogue, such as Rothley Castle and Codger Fort, both built on prominent crags for Sir Walter Calverley Blackett on part of his Wallington estate. Archdeacon Thomas Sharp, rector of Rothbury from 1720 to 1758, had earlier built a round tower now called Sharp's Folly, prominently seen from the south of Rothbury, reportedly to ease unemployment and to provide him with an observatory.

The woodland walk begins near the extraordinary school built by Dr Sharpe at his and his parishioners' expense in 1762, with its central tower rising in three stages. In the top floor was the master's residence. The classroom was reached by an external stone staircase. A small parking space opens onto a gap in the fence, signposted, with a path running down the hill. At once you encounter one of Dr Sharpe's unusual creations: a tall narrow pointed arch that spans a little tributary.

One path crosses over the top of the bridge that the arch forms, and the other goes down to the burn. If you follow the latter, it runs along the stream bank

79 The arched bridge, Hartburn

and widens at a place where there is a wooden seat. Here is the grotto, cut into the sandstone cliff, again including tall thin pointed arches leading into dark spaces.

Outside, the carved cliff face echoes rock-cut tombs in countries like Turkey, on a much smaller scale, even to the extent of having two niches that look ready to house statues, which were of Adam and Eve; this is an interesting connection with the panel of carved wood in the church, brought from Angerton Hall, on which Eve is presenting or tempting Adam with a large apple. Tomlinson, in his *Comprehensive Guide to Northumberland* (reprinted in 1968 by David and Charles), wrote that one of the statues was found lying prostrate in the grotto.

Inside, the main arch leads to a tall rock-cut dome that is corbelled with dressed stone blocks, and this contains a fireplace. Through another tall arch is a narrow passage that runs along the back. Privacy, a fireplace, and screened access to a wide part of the stream which has smooth natural stone bedding through a tunnel make this a discreet changing room with access to modest bathing!

From here the path leads up the hill, with a steep drop to the stream on the right. At the top, the path divides; one continues as an easy route back to the road. The other hugs the top of the ridge behind houses, gardens and small fields where horses are kept, and another surprise is in store. Suddenly the high bank is deeply cut by a wide green track leading down to the burn. The explanation is offered on

80 Hartburn excavated rockface

an inscribed boulder, which declares it as the Devil's Causeway, a Roman road. It is heading for its crossing of the stream on its way north, where we have met it at Rimside and below Caller Crag on its way to Berwick-on-Tweed. It has come from the south-west from Portgate, near Corbridge, in a gate through the Roman Wall, and travelled through Ryal, east of Shaftoe Crags to Hartburn. Generally its course is invisible, represented by a dotted line on a map, but here and on the tarmac stretch from Horton to Lowick it is visible. Tomlinson tells us that the lane was locally known as 'Hurpath', which is interesting because it is like the derivation of Harbottle from Old English *hyra-botl*, the army's or hired people's building; it may mean the army path. Elsewhere its course has to be confirmed by excavation, unless it shows from the air.

From here the path reaches the sharp-pointed bridge (accept the pun if you like) where we started. You may also wander from here along the stream in the other direction to the site of the church.

The church of St Andrew stands high above the stream valley, but the steep drop must have presented problems for the builders to buttress it after it was extended from its possible pre-Conquest beginnings through its early Norman and thirteenth-century developments. The later vicarage is a grand affair, with extensive lawns, its earlier building dating back to the late sixteenth century, but with predominantly

81 Inside the man-made cave

eighteenth-century work now visible on the outside (Pevsner 305). Local historians
owe much to the Rev. John Hodgson, who died there in 1845, aged 65, whose
memorial tablet is in this church, a most appropriate setting. The church has great
interest architecturally, and this interest extends to its churchyard, which has some
of the finest and most numerous gravestones of the eighteenth century in the county
(see Beckensall, 2005). There was obviously a local skilled mason with access to
some fine sandstone.

All these sites, walks and buildings may be accessed from a walled car park close
to the church, just off the main road.

Hartburn has great attraction for us; its church grew from pre-Conquest times and
is full of interest. So is the graveyard, where all the symbols of mortality and hope
for heaven are splendidly carved in stone.

A visit to Hartburn and Middleton may also take in a visit to Shaftoe Crags,
described elsewhere in this book.

There are over 400 'deserted' village sites in Northumberland, documented, and
made available in two PhD theses. Their locations are hidden in documents and old
maps, and those buried under the ground can be seen in some conditions, especially
from the air. A classic example is South Middleton, pictured in this chapter, but many
have much fainter traces.

82 Hartburn church, with its eloquent gravestones

One site recently explored will serve admirably as an example of what may still be hidden: Dr Greg Finch researched the deserted village of Dotland, south of Hexham, and published a summary of his findings in 2008 in 'Hexham Historian', one of the few local publications that has done much to further original research, and a good model for others to follow. Like so many of these settlements, it is not characterised by the ruins of a church or other old buildings, which makes the task of understanding it more difficult. Here is Greg's summary, in his own words (pers. comm.):

Until 20 years ago Dotland Farm stood alone on its hill. It commands fine views to the north, east and south, but lay slightly below the western hilltop, gaining some shelter from the prevailing wind. The Ordnance Survey map, that great source of so many clues to our landscape's past – and still more questions – marks the site of a 'deserted medieval village' in a paddock containing the undulations of long lost cottage and garden walls. Dotland, once the largest settlement between Hexham and the moors to the south did indeed suffer dreadfully in the medieval Black Death, but it recovered, and at least 20 households lived there by the late seventeenth century, surrounded by their open fields and common land. Aerial photos of a snowy landscape help to pick out features that are now hard to see on the ground. A village green sat between humble cottages, the village well at one end and a

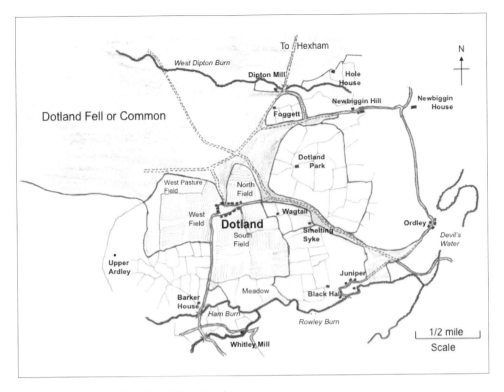

83 Dotland 'deserted' village (Greg Finch)

pinfold or pound for stray animals at the other. Elsdon's village green, far away to the north, still has its pinfold. Dotland's was in decay by 1709, as was the rest of the village. Population fell quite rapidly to just half a dozen households in the next few years, and the open fields were enclosed to create the orderly pattern of fields we see today. Agricultural change had been sweeping Tynedale for decades, driven by the huge growth of Newcastle and its coal industry. Land once farmed in common by small tenants was being enclosed into smaller fields to create more specialised and efficient farms. Open field enclosure was an emotive subject from the Tudor period onwards, and often linked with rural depopulation. Dotland appeared to fit the stereotype, especially as the land was bought and then enclosed by a rich Newcastle lawyer. But, as so often, appearances can be deceptive. We look at the beautiful rolling landscape today, the fields, woods and heather-clad moorland purple in the late summer haze and want to lament the loss of a bucolic self-sufficient little community. Dotland, though, was a desperately poor village, the cottages just draughty hovels giving little protection from the harsh cold of long dark winters. In the decades before its demise the death rate of infants approached the level seen in much bigger, filthy and crowded towns. Rather than being forced out of a rural paradise it is far more likely that people left for somewhere – anywhere – better. The district as a whole was growing in population with the rise of lead mining, rural industry and the continued need for a great deal of labour to work the land. Some people moved just a mile or so away – and prospered. For the smaller number who remained there was continuity – the Simpson family remained as blacksmiths, for example, as they had for generations past. It took more than another century for the remnants of Dotland village to decay into local memory, before being finally swept away by Victorian farm improvements. The world had moved on, leaving little but a few crude courses of roughly worked sandstone in the paddock, the lonely cry of the curlew, and the gentle myth that Dotland had been 'formerly a town'.

What can be seen in this sketch map is summarised by its author:

> The landscape south of Hexham has always featured dispersed farms surrounded by their own enclosed fields, but the few larger settlements had open fields -or 'town' fields farmed in strips. The three fields at Dotland – West, North, and South – were arranged around the village, where the cottages sat around a green crossed by the track to Hexham.
>
> To the north and west lay a large expanse of common or fell land, which can be seen here opening out in a widening strip from the village, allowing direct access to the rough grazing on the fell for livestock from the farmsteads. Similar patterns can be found around other villages in the county. Dotland's open fields were enclosed around 1714, and the fell in 1760, near the start of a long period of common land enclosure across Northumberland in the remainder of the 18th and early 19th centuries.

I know of no better way of ending this chapter, as what is written here shows just how 'hidden' much of our history is, and how it is wrong to generalise about what happened in the past.

It is important to know that just prior to this book's publication (February 2009) Greg's work was recognised by the British Society for Local History, which declared this to be the best article of 2008, 'the overall winner by a large margin'.

6

STONE AND LANDSCAPES

Wherever we travel in Northumberland we are constantly meeting rock formations that have the power to inspire us by their position, shape and texture. Hadrian's Wall attracts many visitors not only because of its historical significance but also because its open landscape is so exhilarating. The central section of the Wall is dominated by the Great Whin Sill, creating a vertical edge of pillars of basalt and a rise and fall that adds considerably to a walk along its course. The Romans used it as a natural barrier, a high line of demarcation between them and the 'britunculi', the 'barbarians' to the north. It is a place where empire halted.

Bamburgh, Holy Island and Dunstanburgh Castles are all built on top of its columns. Thockrington church, as we have seen, takes advantage of whinstone's height.

The Cheviot Hills, with a core of granite and a spread of other fire-formed rocks, generally rounded by the flow of ice sheets, are intersected in places by deep valleys, creating their own kind of rolling landscape.

Most of the county is made up of sedimentary rocks, of the kinds that we see at Howick: sandstone, limestone, shale and coal are widespread and signs of their exploitation are evident everywhere. The sandstone scarps are particularly impressive, forming a prominent sweep of high land overlooking fertile valleys and plains, the steep edge facing into the centre of the county and the dip slope gentler in its path to the North Sea or to the south. Among these are the impressive Simonside Hills, forming steps on the horizon, and their extension north-east past Edlingham. Sandstone in particular produces dramatic shapes, with irregular layers deposited by ancient seas and rivers that become distorted by vast earth-movements, twisted bedding planes creating surreal forms. Faults in the earth's crust create valleys and chasms.

Our route now takes us to Shaftoe to see an example of this, and it is one of many tracks seldom taken. Shaftoe is visible for miles around (for example, from the Hexham-Alnmouth road as it approaches Wallington Hall). It lies close to Bolam and to the deserted village of South Middleton. The track to this high, tilted but generally uniform outcrop is from the Bolam end, and you go there along the dip-slope, at first on a hard farm track past a large prehistoric burial mound to the

84 The Great Whin Sill and Walltown Crags

south, called 'The Poind and his Man'. The mound is flanked by a standing stone, its partner having been taken years ago to become a feature in Wallington garden. On a clear day, Simonside is visible over the top of this 4000 year-old burial mound.

In Northumberland, standing stones are not usually quarried, but are taken as found and then buried upright, with the grooves running down into the earth. The ridges and grooves along the bedding planes exist naturally from the formation of the rock, and they continue to be attacked by weathering, which accentuates the lines and finds their weaknesses. Once they are in position, they become impressive in their stillness and quiet dominance of a site. Many of these have been given names over the years which attribute a function to them that may not have been the intention of the prehistoric people who erected them, such as The Warrior Stone, The Stob Stone (Matfen), or the King's Stone near Flodden; others take on the names of the places where they have been standing for thousands of years: Duddo and Swinburn, for example. They are the stuff of legend.

Grooved stones are found naturally, as we can see at Caller Crag, although people add small details to them, such as cup-marks in prehistoric times. Left to themselves, the rocks are shaped in a way that tempts us to read into them something recognizable, like faces.

85a (right) & *b (below)* Dunstanburgh from coast to castle, and the basalt outcrops

86 The Cheviot Hills: from Gains Law to Yeavering Bell

87 The Poind and his Man burial mound

88 The Matfen standing stone, moved from its original location

89 Goatscrag

90 The Jubilee Memorial stone

Shaftoe Crag marks the edge of the sandstone scarp outcrop. A natural break brings in a track known as the Salters' Road, easing its way through the gap east, and seen in the west following wall and field boundaries. On one side of the track is Jubilee Hill with its triangulation pillar, from which there is an extensive view.

It is called Jubilee Hill because a local man, Mr Atkinson, felt inspired to erect the monolith in honour of Queen Victoria. From here the Simonside Hills, the top of Cheviot and Wallington Hall are visible.

On the other side are the remains of an Iron Age/Romano-British enclosure, its low walls taking advantage of a naturally defended high point.

These lie in an area where there are artificial mounds, too, which could either be for the burial of the dead or for field clearance. Now there is moorland and grazing for sheep and cattle.

As in so many other places in Northumberland, the views from on high are striking. The name Shaftoe first appeared in 1231, and is Old English for a 'shaft-shaped ridge'. This 'ridge' element is repeated in places like Prudhoe, Cambo, Ingoe, and Sandhoe, all of them living up to their suffix. Not far away is Belsay, which, although at first sight not so clearly of that origin was *Bilesho* in 1262, and means Bill's or Bilfrith's ridge. As you find in this book, names carry with them a history of temporary or permanent features within a landscape whether it is long-established towns and villages or more transient field-names.

91 A late prehistoric enclosure

On Shaftoe crag is one of the most remarkable little valleys in the North, broken by faults and smoothed by ice, a place of great variety and mystery. Its rock formations are splendid natural sculptures; although we may delight in the shut-off and attractively inaccessible position, it was home for people over 7000 years ago. There is evidence of habitation in the shelter under the rock overhangs and the ancient remains of later prehistoric people are spread widely over the area.

The bedding planes that we see have been inclined and twisted, with vertical tilting leading to formations that look like organ pipes or fluting. We see this too at St Cuthbert's Cave and at Caller Crag. The process begins with little cup-shaped depressions on top of the rock, where water begins to gather and then run down.

The rocks are layered and time, too, is in layers, for in the area we move from these the earliest people in Northumberland to the Neolithic and Bronze Ages, to the pre-Roman and Roman periods and to the medieval farming systems of rig and furrow ploughing. We are not far from the medieval landscape of Middleton, and we are close to prehistoric rock carvings. There are some minor carvings on Jubilee Hill, but to the north-east, further down the slope, are some little natural ridges that have markings that we have only recently discovered.

It is only very recently that John Davies (2004) and his team have excavated some of these temporary settlements and discovered the flints that enable us to identify Middle Stone Age people. They are roughly of the same period as the people we

92 Faulted and ice-sculpted rock

encountered at Howick on the cliff top, but at Shaftoe they chose to dig deep under a natural shelter for their temporary home rather than live on top of a cliff. Again, here we have an area made exciting not only by natural beauty, but also by the activities of humanity over thousands of years.

There are few things more elusive than traces of the earliest people here, the Mesolithic (Middle Stone Age) people; what we know is generally picked up off the land surface, particularly when it has been ploughed, and in the shelter of rock overhangs. As with other prehistoric cultures, the main sign is the scatter of flint and chert flakes that were the result of their making tools, including barbs for arrows, scrapers for cleaning out animal skins, knives, small saws and stone axes. These little scraps of time are especially valuable when there is no pottery and no obvious evidence of settlement such as huts and walls. Finds of arrowheads and parts of axes may well indicate the use to which these tools were put, and can be 'stray' finds; an animal wounded by an arrow could tail it for miles before it died. On the other hand, concentrations of waste and other stone can show where the settlement was, no matter how temporary.

Mesolithic 'settlements' like the roundhouse at Howick are very rare; recently there has been more to discover under rock overhangs. These are not 'caves', for they do not penetrate very far into the rock, but they provided temporary shelter for small groups; sometimes they were used for the burial of the dead in Early Bronze

93 Faulted and ice-sculpted rock

Age times. An overhang at Goatscrag Hill (Broomridge is its other name) is part of a long scarp which has had burials on top, rock art hammered onto outcrop and ploughed in more recent times; it was used to bury the cremated dead in urns, and on the vertical surface of the interior of the shelter there are carvings of four animals, possibly deer. We do not know the date of these carvings.

Some of the Shaftoe shelters are deeply screened by vegetation, especially by trees, but nevertheless some promising sites have been excavated recently, with a story of temporary sheltered settlements brought to light. The Mesolithic is the period of about 8500-4000 BC. One rock-shelter at Salters' Nick and others have revealed discarded flakes and thin blades, built up by use over many years. Without this attention to detail we would not know this. Add the excavations to intensive field walking, in which all objects found are recorded in their places, and we have a little more hidden history to add to the general picture.

The history of rock-shelters in Northumberland does not end with the Mesolithic. At Ketley Crag on Chatton Park Hill I recorded in detail (three times!) one of the most profusely decorated rock surfaces ever found, with patterns of cups and rings covering the whole surface, taking advantage of the slightly uneven surface to achieve this, perhaps thousands of years after the Shaftoe people were using their shelters in a more basic way; why this particular shallow shelter was chosen, apart

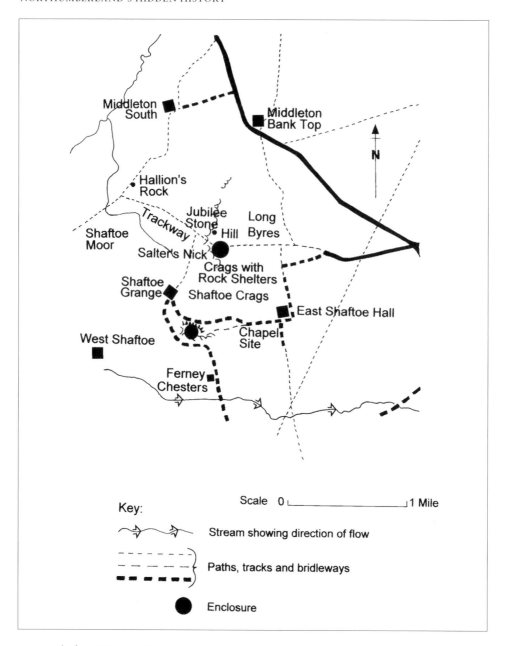

MAP 5 Shaftoe (Maureen Lazzari)

from the incredibly fine view from it, is not known; it could hardly have been used to shelter more than one or two people and that with difficulty, neither does it appear to have had a burial dug into its shallow surface (*colour plate 25*).

This brings me to what used to be of the biggest mysteries in Britain, a truly hidden archive that has now captured the imagination of many researchers, but has long intrigued interested people in Northumberland: prehistoric rock art.

ART ON THE ROCKS

My own discovery of hitherto unknown places in Northumberland owes much to my interest in rock art. Over 5000 years ago, in a long-continuing tradition, people whose view of the world was often expressed in circular images, by building henges out of circular ditches surrounded by walls made from the upcast, circles of wood, ditches and stones, and circular burial mounds were strongly urged by this tradition to mark many places in the landscape with their simple symbolic art. They did this with a hard stone tool (before metal became current), hammering at rock surfaces specially chosen for their dominant viewpoints or nearness to important places like springs. They did not simply impose their images on the 'best' surfaces, but chose outcrops already suggesting the shapes and patterns that they wanted to make, so that natural cracks, water channels, depressions and lumps suggested a design and became part of it.

An outstanding example of this is on Old Bewick Hill, where a large block of slightly tilted, ice-moved, sandstone from which there are extensive views was used for the carvings, taking into the account the natural erosion and basin at the top end of the rock, and adding to the grooves and indentations already there. It is the work of artists who were acutely aware of the possibility of their medium. The

94 Old Bewick: a panel unrecorded until the early nineteenth century

symbolism used is simple, but its arrangement incorporates a meaning that is almost impossible to state thousands of years later. Yet we can enjoy its impressive artistry. How can we really expect to understand fully what people thought when they lived such different lives from ours? It can be arrogance to assume that we know, for we tend to superimpose our own culture and even wish-fulfillment on the past. There was no written record to tell us what we would like to know. Yet we can understand the importance of places for the siting of these motifs, though they would have been limited to what the makers considered to be a workable rock surface. We cannot assume they saw what we can see today, as vegetation has changed, particularly the tree cover which may have blocked off some views and led to the possibility that the art might have been created in woodland clearings. There is a pattern of distribution where marked rocks overlook the lower, more fertile agricultural land on plains and in valleys, the rocks themselves being in 'marginal' areas of thinner soils and vegetation. That in itself shows us that in such areas, mobility would have been paramount; we have a picture of people following game or moving their animals from one pasture to another, via streams and water holes. The farms on the lower slopes and in valleys would have fixed the population more strongly to the land with houses, stockades, and enclosed fields, but upland activities provided an essential part of their needs. Later, the same hill was the place at Old Bewick where a large hillfort was built, marking a need for strong defence, a meeting place for the scattered farmers, and a place where beasts could be enclosed safely; the gap in time between the two cultures can be around 3000 years. It is by comparing sites where all these things happen, such as Shaftoe, with one another, adding detail to detail, scrap to scrap, that the picture of life in the past has gradually built up.

Northumberland has one of the greatest concentrations of rock art sites in Britain, a history hidden from those who live in the South, where rock art hardly exists. It was until recently largely ignored for that reason by intensely parochial archaeologists. Because it has now caught the popular imagination and has been the focus of research programmes involving volunteers too, with web sites that are world-wide and highly respected, it has become popular. Thus it is no longer the hidden knowledge that it used to be!

Northumberland has over 1000 recorded panels and individual stones from outcrop, rock-shelters, earthfasts, rockeries, buildings and burial sites, showing original uses and some recycling. The use of art in burials of roughly the same period, and on standing stones points to another function: that they were used in rituals – a general term which means that they became associated by repeated use with monuments. A clue to such uses is in places for the dead, for in Ireland there are elaborate tombs which exhibit an array of exotic art both inside the mounds and on the kerbstones around them. In Northumberland there are excavated sites of cairns, not necessarily containing burials (for these have been the object of treasure hunters for years), where there are many motifs both in the cairn material and on the outcrop that supports them. Elsewhere some cists (stone-lined boxes) which contained the remains of the dead were either re-used decorated slabs or made especially for the burial. This gives the art form a strong 'religious' use; it is not open to the sky, but hidden from sight – a private matter between the living and the dead. Cairns at Fowberry, Weetwood and Hunterheugh, all in areas of decorated outcrop have recently been excavated, giving more information, but still asking more questions. A programme of targeted excavation would be very helpful so that we can learn more; for example, on Weetwood Moor there is a disturbed cairn near the St Cuthbert's trail, which pilgrims might do well to visit, where the centre appears to have a rifled cist; inside there is a cup-marked stone and outside, the possible decorated cist cover. It is difficult to find, on a slight rise in deep heather. The cairn itself, like that at Fowberry nearby, has motifs on the outcrop on which the cairn is built. There are so many sites that we know which are like this: capable of giving more information at a relatively low cost.

There are not many stone circles in Northumberland, but in Cumbria sites like Long Meg and her Daughters make use of elaborate rock art. The lovely, small circle of fluted stones at Duddo has a possible line of small cups, whereas single standing stones like those at Matfen, Ingoe and Swinburn have a scatter of cup-marks.

Out in the open, we become aware that the marked rocks may follow trails used by these mobile people, so the search for such tracks opens up a wealth of other discoveries; I have found rock art sites in remote places which I might otherwise not have visited, and at the same time found artefacts and sites of many other periods. History is about the whole impact of people on the landscape at all times, and has to be searched for.

At a recent 'rock-event', in which speeches were made, mainly of a 'managerial' nature, right at the end one of the volunteers stood up to give his impression of what the search for, and recording of, rock art, had meant to him. It was a breath of fresh air; his enthusiasm for the places that he had visited, the joy of the search, the mystery with which he had to grapple, the company he found himself in, and the understanding that at the end of it all the mystery would remain, lifted my heart. The sad thing about so much learning is that it becomes sterile and downright boring through the language used and the reliance of scrolls of words on a screen that we would do better to read for ourselves elsewhere. It is such a pity that good research should be so spoilt by taking all the guts out of it to satisfy some standard of presentation which is meant for a very narrow audience. I would prefer to hear talk that may not be word-perfect, that is not read aloud but spoken from the heart, than the slickest of power-point presentations.

So what is there to find that is so stimulating?

The richness of Northumberland's past is not confined to one or two places. This book shows that when a search is made or an established site visited the interest generated is many-layered. When I looked at waterfalls in Chapter 2, the site of Roughting Linn was also a place of prehistoric settlement and of rock art, for here is the largest panel in England.

Over 18m (60ft) of outcrop is covered with images that vary between heavily executed deep groves to delicate, flower like arrangements. Once it was hidden. In the nineteenth century it was cleared of its turf cover when the rock was highly visible, standing out above the vegetation. In time it became hidden by the growth of trees, perhaps encouraged

95 Roughting Linn, recently tidied up, 2008

by the owners, and access became a real problem, especially as it was not sign-posted. It did have a Ministry of Works notice board, which decayed to such an extent that it became embarrassing to think that this was how we displayed our rock art to the rest of the world. In another way the hidden rock retained a lovely magic quality, despite a very clumsy wooden fence erected around it. This year the site has been tidied up, so that the rock is no longer threatened with splitting by tree roots, but it still remains a problem for further management. 'Oh, good, I've seen it, so let's cover it up again', is hardly fair, but there is an important point that if the site is threatened in any way, it must be safeguarded by all means. To hide all would be unreasonable and brutal, so it is important to assess each site carefully and ensure that those completely open to the public are well-managed. This has been done particularly well in the Kilmartin region of Argyll, where the agreed access and sensitive display of information has gone some way to solving the problem. Now the Roughting Linn rock stands clear of tall trees as it did in the nineteenth century, but today one may expect many more visitors.

The spread of Information Technology has made virtual access to all the sites quick and easy, lifting yet more veils. Northumberland has very good Internet coverage of all its rock art, with an international reputation for good recording. However, sites may be difficult to find even with the help of GPS, and continue to hide from potential viewers.

96a & *b* Fowberry cairn when exposed (see also colour section)

A cairn on top of decorated outcrop rock at Fowberry that I excavated in the 1970s is an interesting comment on what can happen. The whole complex was meticulously recorded after excavation, most of the loose marked rocks that made up the double-ringed cairn were stored in museums, with three remaining on site, invisible. As the site is on private land and had been excavated because of the goodwill of the landowner, and because he did not want his special woodland to be invaded by the general public, it was agreed that the site should just be allowed to return to nature. Serious students are still allowed to visit, but the site must not be disturbed. It is a compromise that I find acceptable. All rock art has been entered on a data base, and rocks scheduled as Ancient Monuments; this does not necessarily protect them, though.

There are many marked rocks visible to people on sites when there is much else to see of the past, too. At Lordenshaw, south of Rothbury, there are about 70 marked rocks, some very small, some covered over, some scarcely visible, but there are some that will satisfy the curious. A large, partially quarried block of outcrop with a sloping and indented surface was chosen for a variety of symbols, being at an outstanding viewpoint overlooking the Coquet Valley, Cheviot Hills, and the Simonside Hills. It is anything but hidden, and is visited often, along with cairns, a large hillfort, a Romano-British settlement built into it, ancient fields, a deer park wall, cists, cairns (one built on decorated outcrop rock), deep, numerous quarry tracks, drove roads, a 'shieling' (temporary herd's shelter in the summer), recent rig and furrow, and even an attempt to mine lead. Within such a rich area, it takes a practiced eye and some handed-down knowledge to perceive all of this.

Because I have excavated two cairns there and recorded all the rock art, I have a particularly soft spot for the Fowberry-Weetwood area, near Wooler. I have already mentioned some aspects of the sites, but will use them to show another aspect of the 'hidden' rock art past: that it depends on the time of the day and the time of the year to reveal the art in all its glory. People who view it in dull light often think that it is eroding away, when suddenly a shaft of sunlight will make it all spring to life. My most recent visit was in November, 2008, and the pictures that I offer here tell their own story. Rock art is a visual experience, of course, and the low angle of the autumn sun shows it to perfection. It is never the same: there is always a surprise, elation, or a disappointment in store, but it underlines the value of visiting it often, as well as seeing something else that has been hidden from you previously.

It is easy to concentrate on the more spectacular art, but we must remember that the act of hammering a cup and groove onto a rock could have been an act of great significance.

Further to the west on the same moor, close to a large communications tower, along a well-established footpath, the sandstone outcrops dip all around to a lough. Two of these outcrops have markings, and what is so dramatic is that they seem to pinpoint the importance of water there. It meant that in the deep past herdsmen could lead their animals there to drink in the summer. It meant also that the water would attract wild animals and game birds, so hunters would take up their positions there. It is an area of marsh grasses leading to the lake, and there is a delightful fringe of trees. The approach to this dip in the land does not shout out to be seen; it leads us gently on to the only stretch of water on this large sandstone outlier, making the origin of its name, *mer-tun* a farm by the cold mere or pool. Weetwood itself is the wet wood, and Fowberry the fortified enclosure of the foal.

97a & *b* Weetwood/Fowberry in November 2008

98 Hartley Burn cup-marked stone

To take one area far away from those just described: Hartley Burn, we move further south and to the borders of Cumbria where this rough and rather bleak moorland hides prehistory that includes rock art, cairns and enclosures of the type that were common in pre-Roman and Roman times for cattle. The examples immediately link them with a tradition that extended all over northern Britain. Here, though, the art is not complex, but concentrates on cup marks that are randomly scattered, occasionally with a surrounding ring, or clustered. They are well concealed, and there may be still much to be found.

It is apparent that one of the strongest indications of the use of a landscape in prehistoric times or even the only sign, is the hidden spread of worked stone that often lies in the ploughsoil, revealed by ploughing, harrowing and deliberate excavation. So many of the tools have been found in Britain, and in a datable context, that it is possible to put them in some sort of order of time and use, from the thin Mesolithic blades of Shaftoe through the leaf-shaped arrows of the New Stone Age and the sophisticated barbed-and-tanged arrows of the Early Bronze Age, looking like supersonic aircraft that fly low over Northumberland. Some tools are common to all periods, as the animals had to be killed, skinned, cleaned out and stitched to make clothes and tents as well as eaten. The tools and waste flakes are found in many places; originally they were found in the fertile arable area turned up by the plough, but with the spread of forestry in Northumberland many dense sites

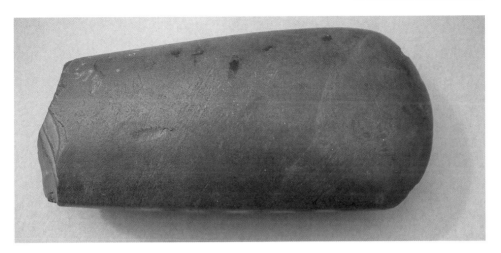

99 A Langdale axe from Great Whittington

were found in disturbed soil and others were excavated in their contexts when sites were either discovered by chance or specially targeted. A good example is the interest generated in the Chatton Sandyford moorland area, where many fine worked flints have been picked up and hundreds of burial cairns have been plotted.

Just north of Hadrian's Wall a stone-mason with an interest in such things was looking at a scatter of stone in a field at Great Whittington when he picked up a superb 'Langdale' axe. Dark green in colour, highly polished and symmetrical, it had been imported from Cumbria, where it was made 4000-5000 years ago at Langdale Pikes, where there is a kind of stone called volcanic tuff which was mined in a high and difficult place, its inaccessibility lending it some sort of awesome quality, for it was so highly prized that the industry to mine and polish it was able to export axes all over Britain, some reaching Europe. Many have been found in excellent condition. The example here was probably broken by farm machinery, but the rest is perfect. The implication is that such objects may have been highly valued for their beauty and rarity as much as their usefulness (status symbols), not only from Cumbria but from anywhere in Britain where a rare, attractive and workable stone was to be found. The large 'bluestones' transported all the way from the Welsh Mountains to form part of the circles of Stonehenge were similarly valued. We must not assume that prehistoric communities were static; they had the means to travel, and the desire to trade. Thus much of the flint found in Northumberland comes from elsewhere, and so do objects of amber and jet.

Whereas in the past these objects were collected as rarities, and often displayed proudly in their owner's homes, more attention is given to recording exactly and systematically where they were found, and more data has led to a fuller picture of the life of the people who made them. It was a technology essential to making a living, but it was also an industry involving luxury goods and cult objects.

The picture shows just a few of these objects found hidden in Northumberland.

So some of our hidden history comes to light, by chance or design, and so much

100 Flint tools from Northumberland

has been discovered recently that it is possible to look at objects found earlier in a new light. Once one set of clues appears, a search for others may find burial sites and habitations.

History can be 'hidden' when we know it is there. There are hundreds of places in Northumberland which could tell us their story, but time and resources, and prudence, cannot allow more than a selection to be excavated. For example, at Dilston, near Hexham, there is a stone chapel and tower that are relics of a Roman Catholic family that became involved in the Jacobite rebellion, which led to the decay of the Radcliffe estate and the deliberate dismantling of a fine late seventeenth-century house that had incorporated a medieval defensive tower. There are pictures and plans of the house, and plenty of information about its owners. Thanks to an enthusiastic group which finds the story fascinating, not only has documentary research been undertaken – a great source of our hidden history – but also an excavation has been funded involving professional archaeologists and volunteers to reveal parts of the demolished building and to investigate the relatively little-known tower. A range of servant's quarters has been opened up, and some fine artefacts of glass, pottery and metals have been cleaned, recorded and put on show, along with very detailed plans of these building foundations. An unknown wall earlier than the present tower lay deeply buried beside it, dated by some early medieval pottery. This is typical of what can be done, and helps to balance somewhat the attention paid to all things Roman to the north of the site; it also draws in more people to share the past and to explore it physically. The estates themselves are well-recorded by the Greenwich Hospital Commissioners, especially with maps that show every field

101 Dilston tower and excavations, 2008

with its name – a truly personal touch. Whereas professional archaeology has dealt increasingly with sites at risk and those financed by developer-funding, independent archaeologists of many different skills can still take part in other interesting work and make their contribution to the total picture.

There has been an upsurge in the use of metal detectors, and although in many cases this has damaged sites and is often motivated by greed, other detectorists are more responsible; the Portable Antiquities Scheme encourages finds to be recorded and a fair price paid for objects of value (of which many have been found) but the trade in unprovenanced antiques is downright destructive. Making money out of unearthing the past is quite different from hoping to learn about how people lived.

More people are interested in the process of excavation as a result of programmes like 'Time Team' and 'Meet the Ancestors'. There is more awareness now that archaeology is not the same as tomb-robbing in ancient Egypt, and has its special discipline and aims. Terms like dendrochronology and geophysics have become household words. Once museums used to be full of static objects; now they change and try to explain the significance of the objects to our lives. They were once musty, dead places, and have become more purposeful.

Of course, much of our knowledge of history comes from documents; prehistory has no such sources, so its study had to develop its own methods. The use of documents goes along with what the trowel can reveal, too. We may know that the graveyard of the Hexham Priory canons is to the south of the choir wall, but the accidental finding of skeletons there in 1990 when BT cable pipes were being laid gave us the opportunity to have them all examined forensically; a picture was built

102 The Old Church wall at Hexham, with its history of change

up of the age at which they died, what their diet might have been like, and their physical development. Some of their names appeared on grave slabs, making their history more personal. Today faces can be reconstructed from bones; battlefield and plague burials tell of the grisly ways in which people met their end. The possibilities of learning from unearthed remains are endless. Add to that the quantities of material discarded in towns and villages, and we begin to build up detailed pictures of how people lived their everyday lives.

Documents continue to be found in unexpected places. I offer as an example a package of material sent to me after a talk I gave: a lady who attended thought that I might be interested in having an old map she had had for 20 years, and when I opened the parcel it had all the farms from Hexham to Haydon Bridge colour-coded, every field marked, and all named in a sales catalogue from Whitehall. It was issued by Greenwich Hospital Commissioners over 200 years ago; these were lands forfeited to the Crown by the Radcliffe/ Derwentwater family. They are now in the County Record Office, that fertile ground for those exploring hidden history.

Neither must we take familiar buildings for granted, as they too hold keys to our past. Recently it was proposed to block out accepted public access to a wall in Hexham which was actually a history in itself: of a church built for the townspeople in addition to the Priory, presumably on the site of an early Saxon church, a rectangular, aisled block that was soon abandoned and used for housing, workshops, rubbish dumps and bread ovens. The wall shows so many signs of re-use, of pointed

103 Alnwick: St Mary's Chantry

arches blocked, one with a window later added and again blocked, and hidden in a shop cellar are the foundations of these arches. The Priory became the town church, and for this reason it survived the destruction during the Dissolution of the monasteries under Henry VIII. The proposal to develop the site was, under pressure, withdrawn. Look at the picture of a chapel wall in Alnwick, which also has a long, similar hidden history.

Meanwhile, the discoveries from the earth as well as above it continue in Northumberland. The sheer quantity of material found at Vindolanda, some like leather in a remarkable state of preservation, has given us important evidence of what people wore, ate, and other details of their lives, once hidden under many metres of earth. This in one of the greatest sources of hidden history of the Roman period, and more will be revealed year by year. It involves great expertise not only by the directors and diggers, but of the scientists involved in interpreting and preserving all the finds. I particularly like the way the site welcomes the public (especially children) and shares finds with them on the spot, making this living history. The latest discovery of fine stone storehouses and granary is accompanied by thousands of small bones and other material trapped under the earth, which will take many months to analyse, but what a detailed picture of life they will give!

Everywhere, as at Shaftoe, we can see the art of dry-stone walling that is most impressive in today's countryside.

104 Shaftoe; an ancient hollow way, The Salters' road

Local quarries provided stone, offering us not only a fascinating view of the cross-section of rock formations, but also, in the case of Belsay Quarry Garden a dramatic chasm left when the stone had been taken away offered the opportunity to create a garden with its own micro-climate.

For generations, all over Northumberland stones have been picked from fields to assist ploughing and crop cutting. Some have been piled into mounds to cover the dead; others have been left in piles on the outside of fields in little clearance heaps. The land has thus been re-ordered so that it can be used for the efficient growth of crops, pasture, or left to itself as set-aside. Two little pre-Roman or Roman enclosures on top of Shaftoe Crag had used such stones for their walls and houses.

This is true of sites everywhere; those in the lowlands may have been taken away by modern farming, but it is in areas like Shaftoe where we have something still visible of the past to visit and wonder at.

As this chapter has been concerned mainly with stone above and below the surface, I wish to end with three intriguing sites that I have shared with others, and yet have no definite information about what they are, why and when.

At Rothbury there is a face carved on stone near a quarry. Even though this is relatively recent compared with others, we still know nothing about who put it there or why. At Wrangham in the north of the county, not far from Roughting Linn, is

105 A sheep stell in the Cheviots, beautifully constructed

106 The face on outcrop near Rothbury

107 An amazing undated carving on a boulder in the Simonburn

108 Wrangham rocks

109 The West Allen hound

an extensive carving in a wood behind a farm, which Dr Aron Mazel and I were the first to report. This has been pictured on the internet but so far no-one knows what it is. Stranger still is the large boulder at the side of a stream at Simonburn which has been pictured in many journals and circulated at the British Museum without anyone having any idea about its period or purpose.

Finally, and most recently, the modification of an old farmhouse and its barn in the West Allen valley revealed the image of a hound with a collar, cut into a large sandstone block as part of a doorway surround, the rest being thin local sandstones; this probably was recycled from another building, and is now safely displayed in the house, where it has became an interesting talking point. It cannot be accurately dated.

When we take unfamiliar paths we are going into an unknown country. We cannot expect to understand what we see immediately. We need to be patient, we need to be modest about the extent of our knowledge and we need to keep open minds and humility. We must also be prepared to share our discoveries, our doubts and our ignorance with others.

7

'THE PATHS OF GLORY LEAD BUT TO THE GRAVE'

People, naturally, have been obsessed with death, the final frontier, the place from which no traveller returns. Fear has led some to pay for a comfortable place in the afterlife; many want to be remembered in this world through ostentatious memorials. All these outward signs remain part of our history, although it has little to do with how people will be judged. The famous line quoted above is one of many reminders that moth and dust corrupt, and that we all come to the same state, equal in death.

The way that folk are given a final send-off is, however, very important, as it shows often the regard with which their lives were honoured, the value placed upon them by survivors. A grave can be an expression of great love.

I have written elsewhere about some of the gravestones in Northumberland, which are an incredible record of our comings and goings. We may see how long someone lived, how many children were born and at what age they died, what occupation the dead person had, where he or she was born. They also reflect the artistic tastes of their generation through the choice of stone, symbols, lettering and inscriptions. Unlike many town and city graveyards, the country villages still retain the tradition of stones packed together, clustered round the churches.

I had neglected until recently that other rarer expression of respect: the mausoleum. We have a particularly fine one near Hexham, just off the A68, near Kilnpit Hill, at a place called Greymare Hill. Known as the Hopper Mausoleum, it is named after the man who had it built, originally for his wife. It stands in a dominant position on a hill which commands sweeping views to the south and south-west, visible from the old Roman road, Dere Street. A remarkable eighteenth-century structure, it is only one use of this site, for close by on the same hill there are graves from an earlier period, and a restored church which stands on the site of a medieval chapel. It is even possible that such a prominent place may have been used for even earlier burials, such as prehistoric.

Today it is reached from a minor road, by gate and footpaths that skirt fields of arable land. Within living memory it was possible to drive a horse and cart up to the graveyard gate, but as there are no longer any funerals held there the church is

110 The Hopper Mausoleum

rarely opened for worship, although it is open to visitors thanks to Historic English Churches.

Built by Humfrey Hopper of Black Hedley in 1752 as a memorial to his wife, it was also to receive his body and details of his descendants in a building erected in a neo-Classical style, complete with niches, statues, pinnacles, iron railings and more. It was restored *c*.1977, but has since been partly vandalised, but remains an imposing monument, accessed only by a signposted footpath.

On the south face, there is a slab with a dedication that has been added to over time, but which tails off – either through erosion or from being left unfinished. This says:

Erected by Humfrey Hopper of Black Hedley in memory of his wife Jane Hodsgon who died February 29th 1752 aged 77.
Humphrey Hopper died ... 1760 aged 85.
John his son died December 16th 1776 aged 70.
Joseph his son died October 1793 aged 86.
Mary Walton wife of Joseph Hopper died ...
Humfrey captain 32 Regement (sic) Foot died at St Vincent August 10th 1765 aged 43.
Nicholas son of Joseph Hopper died February 22 1807. George son of Joseph Hopper died January 24th 1818. Joseph Hopper captain of ship Formosa ...

111 The Hopper Mausoleum

The memorial, built of sandstone, until recently was home to a number of small statues, but some have been stolen. It is outstanding for its time, and Hilary Lees says of it that...

> It was built in the sixteenth century Mannerist style and may be the work of an earlier Humphry (sic) Hopper who died in 1663. It has an arched recess holding two recumbent effigies, and above them are two shell-headed niches with formal statues. A scrolled parchment supports two reclining figures and the whole is topped with an arched cupola with pyramid finials.

Close by, amid a graveyard which has some early eighteenth-century tombstones, is a simple cruciform church built later. Inside it has a central arched roof which covers most of the interior, and is full of box pews.

The graveyard is like many others in the county, but it also has its special features. On a flat slab in the eastern part of the walled enclosure are these words, carved boldly:

> Hear lye the body of Mary Oxlee the wife of William Oxley who departed this life July the 30th Anno Domini 1720.

The wording is spread in such a way that the lines were not well calculated, so the words are split. It is simple and moving, the work of a local carver.

In contrast to that is the burial of a blacksmith, who has an upstanding stone carved on two sides. On that facing east he has images of his trade, including horseshoe and bellows, with this inscription:

> Here lies the body of John Hunter from Black Hedley Woodhouse who departed this life April 10th 1792 aged 86. Also the body of Ann Young his sister of the same place who …

It was common to add to inscriptions the death of another member of the family, to the bottom of the slab. In this case it is partly buried in earth and grass.

The blacksmith was a vital member of any community, and his gravestone shows that time and money was spent on its making. It is also clear that what was called for was some special reflection on his trade, so on the west-facing side we have this:

> My Anvill and hammers lies declind
> My Bellows have quite lost their wind
> My Fires extinct, my Forge decayed
> My Vice is in the Dust all laid.
> My Coals is spent my Iron gone.
> My Nails are drove my Work is done
> My Mortal part rests nigh this stone
> My Soul to Heaven I hope is gone.

Trades and professions are well represented in English churchyards, and an interesting comparison with our blacksmith's is one from Thursley in Surrey:

> My sledge and hammer lie reclined
> My bellows too have lost their wind
> My fire's extinct, my forge decay'd
> And in the dust my vice is laid
> My coal is spent, my iron's gone
> My nails are drove, my work is done
> My fire-dried corpse lies here at rest
> And smoke-like soars up to be blessed.

At Bromsgrove, Worcestershire, two engineers who were killed in a locomotive boiler explosion in 1840 were given a similar 'trade' verse to see them off. It begins:

> My engine now is cold and still
> No water does my boiler fill

My coke affords its flame no more
My days of usefulness are o'er…

These examples are interesting reflections on the age when they were devised, a way of coming to terms with death, with a little humour mixed in. Presumably there would have been reports of such epitaphs in wide circulation. Notification of the trade of the deceased was common, as we see on many Northumberland graves, such as the watchmaker at Newbiggin, and the masons cast around for suitable symbols that represented their trades. Some gravestones were expertly carved, but others were not only produced by rather cruder workmanship, but also it is clear that many could not understand what they were carving. Perhaps the scrap of paper on which the sketch had been made by the customer had not been understood. Thus words are curtailed and continue on the next line or parts of words are placed above the last word, or part of a word, at the end of a line. Just so long as the vital information was there about whose grave it was, some niceties were ignored.

This isolated graveyard creates a different kind of feel from those at the centre of villages or other settlements, especially perched high above the surrounding land. However, before what we see there today, there was a medieval chapel and presumably a graveyard with it, so the tradition of a church and 'God's Acre' in one place were there from the beginning. Today there is a church restored in the nineteenth century, now redundant, but the remarkable crossed stone arch inside has a late eighteenth-century date cut into it. So what we have is three buildings on one spot. A local man rich enough to be able to do so chose the same spot to honour his family. He succeeded in making it visible for miles around.

A constant theme throughout history is the inevitability of death; the threat affects people in different ways. It is unlikely that many people feel assured if they believe in Judgement that they will go to heaven. Some may want to 'go gently into that goodnight', whereas others will 'rage, rage against the dying of the light'. One of the most ghastly episodes in world history was the Black Death, not uncommon, and periodically recurring, but at one stage so devastating that half the population died; this tested people's views to the full. Many believed that the Church had let them down, that God had deserted them, and it didn't matter what your status was in life, for all must suffer. It created an equality that had been preached before: equality in the sight of God, which, from the monuments that the rich built for themselves and their families inside churches and out, the rich did not believe. Priests, like everyone else, died, and there was no one left to give the Last Rites or to bury the dead. It must have seemed to everyone that the world had come to an end.

There is one place in Hexham where there is a Dance of Death painting, four panels painted on wood out of possibly more. These are very rare, but the Internet shows others that survive, should readers be interested. The idea of death being depicted as a partial skeleton, often with a gash where its innards had been taken out, was commonplace, and in these paintings a whole line of people ranging from Pope to a baby were depicted, with death-figures leading them, mostly reluctantly, to the grave in a sinister dance. In Hexham there are four: pope, emperor, king and

112 Hexham: the king in the fifteenth-century Dance of Death

cardinal, the latter looking more like a woman than a man. As in so much death imagery common on later tombstones, death is depicted as the Reaper, with a scythe to cut life down. The message is hardly a hidden one, and the symbolism speaks for itself. On tombstones the hour glass (time passing), skull and crossbones (we'll all be like this when we are dead), book (bible or the record of our lives), snake swallowing its own tail (eternity), may be accompanied by angels, often very crudely made and reduced to a pair of wings and head. To these might be added symbols of trade.

Literature reinforces the message. The medieval play *Everyman*, designed to be played out by local people in the streets, rather than in church, begins with God calling Everyman to make a reckoning of his life. He is unprepared. Death explains his mission, which I re-wrote for a production:

I am Death, to all I am the same;
I know no difference in degrees,
But bring the beggars and the princes to their knees.
It's no good if you shout, or weep, or pray
Now that your time has come – you start upon your way.
If you can find anyone one so hardy
Who will go with you, bear you company,
Go find them now, and bring them to God's throne.

All the things that he has most valued in life desert him, until his half-hidden Good Deeds are left, and after confession, penance, contrition and forgiveness, all is not

113 A grave in Falstone churchyard

lost. Such plays, coupled with the painted warnings of the dangers of hell-fire on the walls of churches, and reminders of the rewards of virtue were ways in which central doctrines were brought home to people. In the Reformation and Civil War period such images were considered idolatrous and were destroyed or covered over. How so many images of the fifteenth century managed to survive in Hexham Abbey is a mystery.

Out of all the examples in Northumberland I will end with a gravestone that is not at all well known, and is hidden often by piles of leaves. In Falstone churchyard to the south of the church by the path is a slab that has a skeleton on one side holding a scythe, its other hand resting on an hour glass on a plinth below. On the other side is a woman with tight belt, hair swept back, one hand on her hip and the other holding a branch from which spring three circular flowers (roses?). Above the panel an angel's head rises above outstretched wings that encompass the whole scene. My picture shows that it is hardly hidden, but some who have not seen it clearly have assumed that the skeleton is holding the woman's hand, but it is not.

Graveyards and monuments carry so much hidden history, with their details of the dead such as families, occupations, ages at death, in a rich archive there to be recorded and understood. Sometimes the grave slabs become recycled, ending up as paving slabs, when families of the dead have died, moved away or lost interest. Some local history societies have undertaken the task of ensuring that such a part of our past is preserved, for this, coupled with written documents, tell us about our past.

8

WHAT'S IN A NAME?

History hides itself in names, yet they are given scant attention, either through ignorance or through being taken for granted. They are so obviously a part of our lives, and our past lives, that they are overlooked.

The English language is a result of our history, containing about 30 per cent Old English and the rest largely Latin through Norman French and a smattering of words picked up in the days of Empire, through the power of America and through advances in science and technology. All of us have names, many of which are actually place-names; some are nicknames and others imported. Today the influence of 'celebrities' on the naming of children is as strong as it ever was. In the Border region, many people took on the names of the local tribal chiefs such as Armstrong, Crozier, Hall and Elliott, acknowledging their loyalties to regional rather than to national leaders.

I am concerned here, though, with our place and field names for what they can tell us about the way Northumberland has been settled. Names are one of the richest sources of hidden history. Almost all of them are post-Roman; as prehistory is largely about the time before written records, this is not surprising, but considering the length of Roman occupation it may seem odd that the Romans left little of these in the landscape. What they called places is rarely encountered, although there are a few sources becoming available like the Vindolanda writing tablets, excavated from deep inside layers of preserved organic matter at an extraordinary depth – thanks to the Romans demolishing one fort before they built the next on top, and to the minerals and water in the soil that preserved organic material like wood and even ink. Survivals of rare pre-Roman names, often called 'British' generally, are the names given to strong landscape features such as rivers and hills. Some civilizations and influences can be swamped to such an extent by invasion and settlement from outside that it is as though the people disappeared. Whatever happened to local people is seldom known – whether they were killed off or absorbed by the newcomers' communities.

A reading of our regional maps makes some elements in place-names stand out, such as a profusion of the elements 'ham', 'ton', 'wick', but there are many names that will be a puzzle. The reading of these maps will include sites like 'hillfort', 'settlement' 'quarry', 'disused railway' alongside the symbols for these things, but names are scattered everywhere. So where do we begin? Fortunately much work has already been done for us by generations of scholars, and there are reputable dictionaries of names to consult. The analysis is usually done by dividing names into elements. Ford is one, Berwick is two, and Eglingham three. It is no good guessing what a name means; the crucial thing is the recording of its earliest spelling and changes to that spelling. This enables us to see what the elements are, and, from that, what they mean. So Ford is precisely that – a ford across the River Till; Berwick means barley farm; Eglingham is a farm or settlement established by the people who followed a man called Egwulf. All these elements are Old English, brought in by the descendants of those early raiders who preyed upon the relatively weakly defended coast of the remains of the Roman Empire, who returned at first to Scandinavia and north Germany with booty, and eventually decided that it was a good place to settle permanently. Of course, this took many years, until Northumberland became 'Anglian' with its own hierarchy, ready for war against other Anglo-Saxon kingdoms, a rivalry that ended when William of Normandy brought his knights across from France to conquer England and to establish his lords in positions of power. They would have called most places by their Old English names, with variations in spelling; many regions had these recorded in the Domesday Book – a thorough bureaucratic record of what he had conquered, but Northumberland was so devastated that it did not extend here.

What we have today is the result of centuries of changes to the landscape, but many of the old names remain. People continue to use them without considering what they mean or wanting to change them. That someone lives in Hexham is enough, without considering how it originated or what it means; that is the general approach. The great thing about names is that they tell us what sort of land was conquered centuries ago by those north European pagan warriors. For my book on this (2006) I arranged names, once their meanings were known, into categories, beginning with those that tell us about physical conditions. What follows is a selection from these.

The Cheviot Hills are the highest part of the county to the north-west, but many of their names are not very old. Humbleton Hill means that it was bare-headed, and Clennell is 'clean' in the sense that there was little vegetation on top. In the case of Humbleton this is confirmed by the fact that it has prehistoric cairns and a hillfort on top. It is possible that the delightfully named Skirl Naked was also clear on top and shone in the sun. Elsewhere Plenmeller is also a bare hill.

There are many ways to describe hills and ridges. 'Law' (*hlaw*) is local and means a hill or burial mound; 'dod' also is a hill. Ryal is a hill that grew rye. 'Don' is also common, or 'dun', as it persists in Scotland as a fort on a hill. When we look at a name like Dunstanburgh we see three elements that mean hill-stone-fortification, referring to the earlier and present structures on top of the basalt cliffs. Sometimes a mistake in spelling confuses 'dun' and 'don', the latter being a valley. Warden Hill should be a look-out hill. Rises in ground may be minimal, but Sharperton has a sharp edge, Shaftoe is a ridge, Snook Bank was once *Shakelzerdesnoke*, meaning a ridge on which a shackle-yard stood. Eshott was a ridge covered with ash trees. Druridge is a dry ridge because it was covered with sand dunes.

High places sometimes have the prefix *hea*, high, as in Heaton, and Howick. There are rocky cliffs and ledges: Carraw, Knaresdale, Horncliffe, Shitlington, and other names where 'heugh' appears. Hangwell and Coe are overhangs or rock-shelters.

The shapes of physical features are well represented in names like Cambois (pronounced cammus), meaning a curving bay; bends in streams occur at Crookham. Nesbitt is nose-shaped, Helm is shaped like a helmet, and Spindlestone is spindle-shaped.

When we come to look at names that are concerned with water, there are many to consider.

Waesse (OE) is a wet place or swamp, as at Allerwash, where alders grew. *Eg* is an island in marsh. One element in Ponteland indicated this, an island in the River Pont, perhaps where it was marshy. Fens abound, as in Fenham, Fenwick, and Matfen. There are many references to the fens that provided the stuff of mystery in 'Beowullf', where dwelt the enraged God-hating duo of Grendel and his mother. Much land since its early settlement had to be drained, and this provided rich soil in many cases. However, far from being a barrier to progress, marsh land also provided a bonus if the form of creatures that could be hunted, trapped and eaten. Settlements were set up on the edges of fenland: Morwick and Moralee, for example. Weetwood is the wet wood, Slaley and Swarland are heavy to plough, perhaps because of wet clay soil. Slaggyford was heavy and soggy, and Philip was foul.

Mor (OE) can either be barren or waste land, as in Morwick. *Halh, healh* (OE) is common in Northumberland, usually in the dialect form of 'Haugh' (pronounced 'hoff or 'harf'). Although its general meaning is a corner, a nook, here it is closely related to alluvial land on the sides of a river. In the north it is associated with water, so the Tyne valley haughs make it clear that what is referred to is the large expanse of flat land that separate Hexham from the River Tyne. *Halh* is common in place-names and field-names in England, and its meaning varies with its location, such as dry land in a valley or in a marsh, as in Etal (Eata's or grazing pasture), Humshaugh (Hun's), Hepple, Bothal (Bota's), Broomhhaugh, Greenhaugh, Kirkhaugh (church) and Barhaugh (barley).

Valley names are numerous. 'Hope' is generally a blind valley: Milkhope is an example. Langhope is long and Chattelhope is kettle-shaped.

Water was life, and rivers provided food, a highway for exploration and access, and their names endured even though some of their meanings became obscure. Many were taken over by the Anglo-Saxons from the British, and in some cases the elements *ham, ton* and *wick* were added. There were many different words for water courses; there may have been too much, too little, emphasis on where it came from, where it went, how it flowed, and how deep it was – all things to be taken into account by good farm management.

A standard name for river was OE *ea*, ON *a*, referring to water that was bigger than a brook or stream. Hexham was established at *Hagustaldes ea ham*, the river being the Tyne, of British origin, meaning something like 'dissolve' or 'flow' – the same as in River Till. Other major rivers such as the Aln and Alwin (and the Allen) have equally old recorded names, but we cannot be sure what they mean.

Blyth is pleasant, Breamish may have roared, and Kielder was violent, the Derwent is named after oak trees, the Glen is clear water, and the Tweed is powerful. Other pre-Roman names hiding their meanings are the Maggleburn, the Nanny River and the Irthing. We know what Coquet means: the cocks' wood, presumably after the game birds that were attracted there, but an earlier form means that it was a red colour. The River Reed is red, from iron in the soil. The Wansbeck, another major river, may be named from a causeway made of brushwood. Among streams is the Devil's Water, which is black, while the Erringburn is silver. Holborn is deep, Sleekburn muddy, the Warren has alders, Ritton is small.

Streams flow from springs, the latter being recorded as 'wells', more common in settlement names than 'stream'. Weldon is a fine example, as it also shows how imagination takes over; there is a story of Scots raiders being unable to find Brinkburn Priory in fog, but when the monks joyfully rang their bells of deliverance, the Scots returned, sacked the priory, returned to their leader who thanked them with 'well done, lads'. It is, of course, the place where a spring empties its water into the River Coquet. The element *celde* for spring is rare, and not to be confused with *helde*, which means a slope, as in Learchild, or Akeld.

A name for a stream is 'beck', but this is rare in Northumberland, although common in Cumbria. *Burna* (OE) is more usual, with many elements describing its surroundings.

The joining of streams is evident in Mitford, where *gemyth* (OE), its first element, means a junction. Twizell has a similar meaning, but with a different root, *twisle* (OE), meaning a fork, a meeting place.

Other names for watercourses include *fleot*, *fleote*, referring to an estuary, inlet or small stream. Fleetham is on a small stream that drains into the sea at Beadnell.

Old English *mere* is a pond, pool or lake. One very important place is Coldmartin (*mere-tun*), where in prehistoric times the source of water was essential to upland grazing in the summer. Boulmer, on the coast, was the bull's mere.

Old English *pyll*, *pull*, and *pol* may have been Welsh originally. At Powburn it seems to apply to a slow-moving stream, part of the River Breamish, that forms pools in the gravel deposits, and has become a major gravel quarry area.

There are names for minor watercourses that appear especially in field names. 'Letch' is common – a slow-moving water channel that may be dug for drainage, originating in the Old English *laecc*, *laecce* – a stream or bog. A *sic* (sike) is a small stream and appears in field names too.

Water and marsh are frequently occurring features of the landscape, and are dominant. Not surprisingly, fords, bridges and causeways are the means of crossing them. A causeway was also a means of crossing water or marsh. Causey Park is an example. The River Wansbeck suggests that a brushwood causeway was constructed to assist the passage of wains or wagons.

The term 'ford' is seldom used on its own, though it was on the Till. Mostly it is used as a second element, as at Bradford (broad), Stamford (stone), Styford (the road that crossed it), and Barrasford (by a grove).

When the Anglo-Saxon invaders arrived, they were not coming into a pristine wilderness, but to a well-developed agricultural landscape. The kinds of crops and areas of waste, fenland and moorland were self-evident, and a preponderance of a particular woodland, the amount of good grassland and other features would have made it possible for them to fell trees for houses and stockades, to feed domesticated animals, to allow them hunting and fishing as they had done in their homelands. The most valuable resource was arable farming, hand in hand with stock-raising. Crops of hay for winter feed were essential. The use of upland pastures, seasonally, was also essential.

The place-names give us some idea of what conditions were like for natural growth and for crops.

Forest and woodland were of crucial importance to the economy. Homes and farm buildings and some fences were timber-built. Wood was used for fires, for charcoal-burning, boat-building and for small bridges. The forest was also a food supply for gatherers, hunters and for animals such as pigs and deer.

Clearings in the forest or woods were important, for these became pasture and later ploughed. It is a matter of debate how far Anglo-Saxon settlement was built on existing Romano-British sites, although this would seem the logical thing to do, and how far use was made of new clearances. Clearances were a means of providing new land for new wealth and for an increased population, so if the demand decreased (after the Black Death, for example), cleared land would become colonised by scrub and trees.

A grove was land overgrown with brushwood, known as a 'strother' locally. Strother is also a modern surname. Bolam, another surname, is the place where there were tree trunks, and Stobswood is tree stumps.

Some elements show where woodland was situated. *Hangra* (OE) was a wood on a slope. *Hyrst* (OE) was a wooded hill. It is probable that individual trees captured attention when names were being given, as they could attract legends, mark places where things happened, or be associated with a particular person. But trees in general are named after their kind, showing us what was growing then. The most common were apple, oak, ash, alder, birch, elm, hazel, pear, hawthorn and willow.

Aespe (OE) is aspen, as in Espley, *berce* is beech, in Bockenfield, and *ellern* is elder in Elrington.

One of the most important trees and bushes was the hawthorn, for its resilience and rapid growth. It was a good barrier in enclosures, and Hackwood was thus formed.

The woods themselves were *widu*, *wudu* (OE); Witton confirms the earlier form, *widu*. The word occurs in Woodburn, Woodhorn, Weetwood, Lipwood, Harewood and Coquet (*cocwudu*). In the wood there may have been an outlaw, as in Ratchwood (OE *wrecca*). Scrainwood may have housed either villains or shrews (OE *screanwena*).

Encroachments into the woodland to provide more land for pasture and cultivation produced the *leah* (OE), which can mean forest, glade or clearing, the first step in its cultivation. Eventually these areas became known generally as fields, leazes being the plural of lea, and giving its name to one end of the Newcastle United football stadium as well as the name of the street where I live. At the end of a name, 'ley' signifies a field (ley-liners have adopted this term), with an indication of what was in it, such as: Lambley, Horsley, and Callaly (calves). Clearings themselves became known as 'ridings' from OE *rodu*, as in Riding Mill. If a field is called by that name, it is most likely to refer to a clearance rather than to horse-riding, if it is old.

Small woods were *sceaga*, which became 'shaw' as in Shawdon and Ellishaw, but this must not be confused with a ridge.

Names included wild birds and animals: wildcat, wolves, fox, badger, otter, crane, crow, woodpigeon (cushat), owl, eagle, hawk, blackbird (ousel), sandpiper, heron, raven and woodcock. Wild goats give their name to Yeavering Bell, still there, as well as to Gateshead. Hunted animals include hare, hart (stag, deer); game birds, too, were hunted.

Bees could have been wild or kept. There were domestic animals: calves at Callaly, and Callerton, sheep, a foal, horses, geese, swine, heifers and cows. At Cullercoats doves were kept in dove cotes or 'doocats' as local pronunciation would have it, as an extra source of meat in winter.

Anglo-Saxon personal names form a large part of place-names. Without them, we might know nothing of many of those people. Most appear as first elements, naming a settlement or landscape feature, and some names appear relatively frequently. Here are some examples:

Pauperhaugh (Papworth), Pegswood (Pegg), Pigdon (Pica), Prendwic (Prenda), Prudhoe (Pruda or 'proud'), Rennington (Regna), Rochester (Hrofi or *broc*), Rosebrough (Osburh), Rothbury (Hrotha), Rudchester (Rudda).

When we come to the places where people lived and farmed, the original field was *feld* (OE), as in Felton, and means large cleared spaces, or open country. Thus it would be treeless, without buildings, level in hilly country and free of marsh, and used for pasture. In the second half of the tenth century this term was associated with large areas of cultivation that produced food by ploughing, sowing and harvesting. It was organised into strips, ploughed communally. It becomes associated as a name not just with open land but with ploughland. Its use as a first element is rare, and is mainly used as a final element after a description of its size, shape, surface, position in the land, and colour. In Bitchfield there are birch trees, and in other names it can belong to someone or have wild creatures living there.

Where the element *land* (OE and Norse) is used, it is land, an estate or new arable. The later the term is used, the more casual its use. In field names it is used to name a strip in the open-field system, or just a piece of ground. Sometimes there is a specific reference to its use. Buteland, for example, is at the limit of cultivation, flanked by high moorland. Coupland meant that it was purchased (ON *kaupland*). If the landowner's name precedes it, if it is ancient, 'land' is most likely to be cultivated, as in Dotland.

Sometimes the land is heavy to plough or wet, as in Swarland.

It is against this background of wild and agricultural land that we see some traces of places where people lived. Early houses would have been made of wood. The sight of crumbling Roman stone buildings with the remnants of heating systems must have been awesome to people who lived in wooden huts. We know from archaeology the structure of some of these, such as those with their bases dug into the earth, or the fine buildings of King Edwin's palace at Yeavering.

Most settlements remained as farms and did not develop much, but villages became the focal point for trade and meetings, as well as the church later. There always had to be a focal point, provided in prehistory, for example, by henges, stone circles and hillforts. By late Saxon times the villages had open fields with arable and mixed farming, and the more ancient farms must have remained scattered outside. In the north the two-field 'runrig' system was in operation, based on an infield nearest the village and an outfield of common pasture. In both fields there are strips and stints, the allocation of land for arable and pasture for the people living there. The three-field system was more usual, with one of the fields allowed to lie fallow so that it could regenerate. There was also watermeadow, woodland and waste shared by all.

These arrangements are best seen in specialized field-name study.

Within this landscape a lonely croft was singled out, Ancroft, much later to become a plague-hit village.

Botl signifies stone buildings, in the case of Harbottle a castle built after the Norman Conquest. One farm, Trewick, is built of wooden posts. New settlements and new buildings are marked, and these appear also in field-names. Yards and enclosures of different kinds – walled, fenced and hedged – are there, and a common element is the shieling, a name given to a temporary settlement for herdsmen during seasonal grazing.

Colours that are outstanding enough to cause comment appear in names which include black or dark places, perhaps with additional connotations, such as forbidding, frightening, applied to hills, valleys and dark heather.

White, on the other hand, may indicate brightness, as at Vindolanda, and names including white may draw attention to some vegetation growth, such as cotton-grass or other grasses that turn white at the year's end in fields, hills and valleys, and Blanchland, from French meaning 'white' refers to the colour of the land in Normandy, *Blanchelande*, in 1165. Fallow or multicoloured is applied to some open lands, valleys and hills.

The size of fields, settlements and fords is present, too.

In addition to Blanchland, other borrowings from French can be a first element, as the word 'beautiful' is applied to a feature. 'Causey' is a causeway, Plessey is an enclosed park. Some place-names are imported with the families who gained land in England, as at Darras Hall, Haggerston, Seaton Delaval, Gubeon and Vauce.

The final selection of names must include references to some aspects of local history. Many ancient sites encountered by early settlers were named. Some were fortified, and this accounts for the number of 'chesters', which applies either to Roman or pre-Roman sites, and the element 'burgh'. Some were abandoned, as we see in those inhabited by crows.

Standing stones, which must have been visible at the time of the Anglo-Saxon settlement, were certainly added to names at a later date, but among the early ones are Fourstones, although the stones are no longer there. A Neolithic burial mound of the 'cromlech' type in which the burial chamber of three standing stones on which a big capstone was balanced was constructed inside a long mound, seems to be the explanation for Featherstone. Other burial mounds, still in the landscape, some of them excavated, belong to the Early Bronze Age and still have the name Hepburn and Hebron to attest to their height and holiness. In the case of Hepburn near Chillingham, a cluster of such mounds overlooks the site of others on Old Bewick Moor. Harlow Hill is the people's mound. Kirkley is Crick's mound or a hill.

There is a puzzle in the location of Gloster Hill, south of Warkworth, for, sharing its name with the more famous Gloucester in the South, no fort has been located there. However, a Roman altar came to light, so this may be a clue to a vanished site. Archaeologists must always be aware of such clues from many sources, of which place-names are one.

Among special places in the landscape, some were meeting places; the rare Dingbell Hill is thought to be a place of assembly, a Norse term.

Details of ownership including land belonging to the king, to priests, monasteries, noblemen, free peasants, a reeve, a named person, appear, as well as those that have attracted some sort of reputation for hiding outlaws and villains, or as places of execution.

Places may have served as look-out hills, prominent boundaries, or the end of a wall or ditch. They may be named after industries, such as limekilns, charcoal-burning, coal pits, salt and mills in addition to all those that we have seen marking fords and other crossing places of rivers and streams.

In Coupland we gather that the land was bought; elsewhere there is disputed ownership and the presence of squatters. There are indications of the large open-fields and their division into smaller units for farming such as furlongs. Clearings, 'ridings' are included, and enclosures.

When we turn to field names, there is considerable reinforcement of these elements, but the study is far more flexible

Why should a field be called Botany, Buttony or Botany Bay, or another Labour in Vain, or another Canada? Field-names change rapidly; for example, when a farm

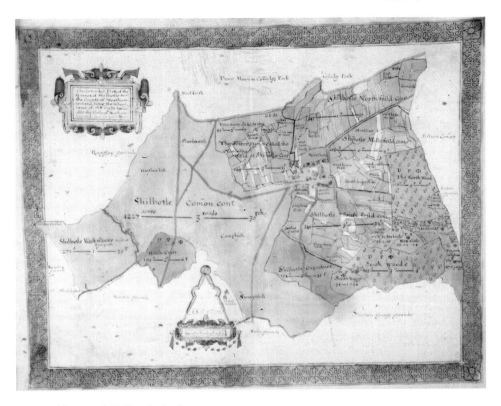

114 Field map of Shilbottle in the 1620s

changed hands, a field name map may be lost, and the new farmer may decide to put in his own. Many still use old names without knowing what they mean, but it does not matter because everyone knows precisely which field is which. Merely numbering the fields would take all the fun out of it, for field names are so intensely personal that they can refer to events that took place there, jokes, comments on the fertility of the soil or difficulty of ploughing it. Even established field-names can be altered in a lifetime; for example, at Eshott a name was changed to March Brown, because a retired colonel of that name who marched everywhere used it as a regular walk, and another was called High Seas because the farmer and his life looked down from a ridge and saw the barley with the wind blowing through it. One could never guess this, and that advises caution. Others like Labour in Vain and Botany Bay were remote and hell to work – like an imposed exile. Klondyke on the other hand may have promised riches from its fertile soil.

Once we have plotted the modern names on a map, the next step is to search documents to find if there is anything earlier, to make a comparison. Some names prove very old, but seldom as old as the place-names. Often the survival of an old map is because it belonged to a big estate, such as those owned by the Duke of Northumberland, which formed a very important source for my work, especially the hand-painted maps of Thomas Norton in the early seventeenth century, or the Greenwich Hospital maps of the early nineteenth century. On two occasions I have been given valuable maps which I then placed in the County Records Office permanently, which shows that more may be lying around. Documents other than maps, involving landholdings for example, are also invaluable.

The result of all this is a picture so rich and rare of the past that it can be breath-taking. I offer just a few examples to emphasise the hidden history to which persistence and scholarship can bring life – what I like to think of as a Breughel landscape: Grimping Haugh, Cork Leach Lay, Hot Bog, the Niddles, Armourer's Fall, The Boiling Riggs, Horners, Corney Horners, Bodle Hole Quarter, Blakehopesburnhaugh, Crum Roods, Fiselbee Pasture, Hungerfull lases, Haughslopp butts, Moralees, Seggy Hole, East Toddles, Horselawpule, le Stobithorn, Faltemere, Korhilles, lez hevelandes, Great and Little Sloshes, Poned lands, Alger-furlang, Allery Bog, Jill's Arse, Bainshaw Bogs, Crookitt roods, Jenny's Darg, Dirt Pots, Saughy Pond, and the Bullion.

Some names includes clues to how the land was sub-divided in the past: furlong, fursheth, furshott, and flat, balks, headlands, acre, land, rigg, selion and dale are such sub-divisions of the common fields, and butts are what are left over. These persist even on modern maps.

The lynchets and terraces of the Cheviot Hills, crossed by downward-running rig and furrow, fossilised because they were allowed to grass over after the loss of fertility of arable land long ago, remain as an incredible ancient farming landscape, visible not only from the air, but brought to life below by slanting sunlight. Together with the names, the history of farming and settlement is there to be read.

9

THE TRACK NOW TAKEN

Exploring landscapes is full of possibilities; there is a chance to encounter something that will attract the eye, move, and possibly uplift, the spirit. A lifetime is not enough to explore all that we should like to see. We may not have the same persistence or focus of a Wainwright, who set his sights on describing his adopted Lake District in precisely 13 years and managed to do so with great skill, insight and appeal. He was unusual, though, as he chose landscapes rather than people; his relationship was with places rather than with flesh and blood.

My book began with a more modest aim: to reveal what I had discovered outside the usual tourist areas of Northumberland by following paths, tracks, and minor roads to places that I have found fascinating. I have not done this as a solitary activity; others have added considerably to my knowledge and to my appreciation. Others may have gone there before me. I have written about only a few places; there is a wealth of further exploration ahead. There always is. There is also a need to revisit constantly places that have proved so interesting the first time. Weather and seasons change, and so do places, and so do we as we grow older, so that we see and experience places differently. There is always something we have not noticed before. Many people can live in the same place and become so used to it that they no longer see it, taking things for granted, having no curiosity.

Robert Frost's *The Road Not Taken* applies to the whole of our lives. Choice, however, is limited and how we exercise it determines what kind of people we are and what we become. The inspiration of the moment, perhaps the result of reading or hearing something that moves us, a work of art, a piece of music, an experience of horror, an accident, an illness, can be pivotal in our lives. A good, inspirational teacher, may cause us to share his or her enthusiasm so that it becomes a part of us, and may even change our lives. Neglectful and cruel parents can stunt our growth. Love can save us or destroy us.

'For good or for ill, let the wheel turn' is a key element in T.S. Eliot's play *Murder in the Cathedral*: destiny and who or what controls it. In some philosophies 'destiny' can mean that we are at the mercy of external forces over which we have no control.

'Kismet', 'Fate' looms over us; we are doomed. The Athenian playwrights of the fifth century BC are vitally concerned with what and why things happen to us. For some, when we get above ourselves, putting ourselves on the same level as, or even above, the gods (the sin of 'hubris' or pride), we are asking for trouble. Shakespeare makes the blinded Gloster in *King Lear* put it this way:

> As flies to wanton boys, are we to the gods,-
> They kill us for their sport.
> (Act 4 sc 1)

Those capricious, all-powerful, vengeful, competitive gods on Mount Olympus played out their fantasies, lust and love of power, through humans down below. Paris is offered the choice of three of their goddesses to award one the golden apple, and this results in the Trojan War in which they all intervene at different times. Was there no escape for Oedipus when it was ordained that he would unwittingly murder his father and marry his mother? There was certainly a note of rebellion that crept into the drama of the day: do these all-powerful beings deserve our respect? One conclusion of one dramatist was that things were so loaded against humanity that you cannot call anyone happy until he is dead and takes his happiness to the grave with him. We have to have a choice to be fully human, but must exercise that choice with the greatest of care and consideration.

The 'track not taken' is both a reality and a metaphor. Literally, as we explore the countryside we have the power to leave the familiar, the well-know, the tried and tested, and seek we know not what. A place can only exist for us when we go there, not by looking at it on a map. From there we can branch out into other parts, learning and experiencing sights, sounds, and smells as we go along. In learning more about places and their history, we learn more about ourselves. All the time we are reacting, thinking, learning to understand the significance of what we see. It is comforting to follow a familiar path, but we may be left with the uneasy feeling that we are missing something. 'What if?'

That is the physical reality of choosing a path. To do what we are told without question, to act as though there is no choice, is an avoidance of what it means to be human. Those who chose the monastic life on Holy Island or who saw the creation of an illuminated copy of the Lindisfarne Gospels as the most important part of their life's work had made a decision that excluded many other aspects of life, such as a wife and children. Saint Cuthbert on the Farne Islands decided that it was only by being physically shut off from the world that he could at times become closer to God. Heaven forbid that we should all choose such isolation, but that was *his* choice to enable him to carry out his mission; it worked for him, and his mission spread. The road of self-denial may not be for all of us. The rich man who confronted Jesus when he asked the master what he must do to inherit eternal life, was given the stark answer: 'Sell all you have and give it to the poor'. He went sadly away. We tend to accept a watered-down version and give something to charity, support good causes, perhaps attend an anti-poverty rally, but that falls short of the demand even if it makes us feel a little better.

Choosing a way is not necessarily a huge decision made once in a lifetime, once and for all. For most of us it is rather like a walk where there are many paths, taken only occasionally, but nevertheless involving small decisions. But what are small decisions for us may affect others enormously. We can be unaware of how much power we have to influence other people, or for them to influence us.

Sometimes we like to pretend that we have no choice at all; an excuse not to have to make a decision. 'They' know better than we do. It is 'their' job to sort it all out. So we keep our heads down, wanting to believe the lies about weapons of mass destruction existing in Iraq or accepting that we must renew Trident at an enormous cost in the hope that it will somehow protect us in the future. It soon becomes obvious that 'they' are not infallible in the way they come to a conclusion and that 'we' have to take responsibility. Those people who protested by words and actions at Druridge Bay were exercising a choice about the situation they saw there, and they succeeded in saving a stretch of the Northumberland coast from exploitation. Official decision-makers can get everything so wrong.

One of the great moments in Mr Eliot's *Murder in the Cathedral* is when Thomas a Becket realises that all the paths open to him are temptations, and at the end of his self-analysis 'the last temptation is the greatest treason: to do the right deed for the wrong reason'. He had been thinking that his forthcoming martyrdom would bring glory after death – his greatest temptation was the very pride that had enabled him to resist the other Tempters. He realised that he had to surrender his will completely so that he desired nothing for himself.

This, then, is the consequence of choice. We may not be called upon to do anything so earth-shattering and heroic, yet all the decisions, large and small, that have been made by so many people are what we call 'history'. Choices may be limited, but all of us in a small or large way are called upon to make them, and the road we take makes all the difference.

BIBLIOGRAPHY

Beckensall, S. 2001 *Northumberland: the Power of Place* (Tempus)

Beckensall, S. 2001 *Prehistoric Rock Art in Northumberland* (Tempus)

Beckensall, S. 2003 *Prehistoric Northumberland* (Tempus)

Beckensall, S. 2005 *Northumberland: Shadows of the Past* (Tempus)

Beckensall, S. 2006 *Place names and field names of Northumberland* (Tempus)

Beckensall, S. 2007 *Hexham* (Tempus)

Beckensall, S. 2008 *Northumberland from the Air* (The History Press)

Beckensall, S. 2008 *Unquiet Grave: A Novel for Young People* (Powdene, Newcastle)

Blair, P.H. 1977 *Northumbria in the days of Bede* (Golancz)

Davies, J. 2004 'Lithics and small finds from the Bolam and Shaftoe region of southern Northumberland', Northern Archaeology. Vol. 20

Finch, G. 2008 'Dotland deserted', The Hexham Historian No 18 (Hexham Local History Society)

Helvenston, P.D. and Bahn, P.G. 2005 *Waking the Trance Fixed* (Wasteland Press, USA)

Kirby, D.P. (ed) 1974 *Saint Wilfrid at Hexham* (Oriel Press)

Lees, H. 2000 *English Church Memorials* (Tempus)

Pevsner, N. et. al. 1993 (2nd Ed) *Northumberland* (Penguin)

Rollason, D. 1989 *Saints and Relics in Anglo-Saxon England* (Blackwell)